Common Threads
of Practice

Common Threads of Practice

Teaching English to Children Around the World

Katharine Davies Samway
Denise McKeon

Editors

Teachers of English to Speakers of Other Languages, Inc.

Typeset in ITC Century and Belwe by
World Composition Services, Inc., Sterling, Virginia

Copyright © 1993 by Teachers of English to Speakers of Other Languages, Inc.
(TESOL).

All rights reserved. Copying or further publication of the contents of this work are not
permitted without permission of TESOL, except for limited "fair use" for educational,
scholarly, and similar purposes as authorized by U.S. Copyright Law, in which case appropriate notice of the source of the work should be given.

Helen Kornblum *Director of Communication and Marketing*
Ellen Garshick *Copy Editor*
Cover design by Ann Kammerer

Teachers of English to Speakers of Other Languages, Inc.
1600 Cameron Street, Suite 300
Alexandria, VA 22314 USA
Tel 703-836-0774 • Fax 703-836-7864

ISBN 0-939791-47-1
Library of Congress Catalog No. 93-060397

Contents

Acknowledgments   vii

1. Common Threads, Common Bonds   1
   Denise McKeon and Katharine Davies Samway

2. For a Brighter Future: SPEAK Project in Soweto   7
   Pippa Stein

3. The "Essence of Sliding": Encouraging Elementary ESL Students to Become Creative Writers   20
   J. Wesley Eby

4. Watson and Son's EFL Class: Teaching English to Chinese Children Using Only English and a U.S. Peer   32
   Tim Watson

5. Teaching English in Russia   40
   Alevtina Poliak

6. Teaching English in Primary Schools in Brunei Darussalam   47
   Ng Seok Moi and Wendy Preston

7. Learning English Naturally in Emelie Parker's Classroom   57
   Sue Sherman

8. How Do They Learn to Read and Write? Literacy Instruction in a Refugee Camp   67
   Lauren Hoyt

9. Team Teaching in Second Grade (Don't Pull Out the Kids, Pull In the Teacher)   78
   Carlyn Syvanen

10. English in Austrian Primary Schools   86
    Maria Felberbauer

Contents

11. Teaching English to Children in China **93**
    Bi Qing

12. Primary Education and Language Teaching in Botswana **99**
    Lydia Nyati Ramahobo and Janet Ramsay Orr

13. A Tale of Two Cultures: At Home in the German School Washington **110**
    Donna Stassen

14. Teaching English in Estonia: Using Reading and Writing Process Methods to Teach EFL **120**
    Emma Wood Rous

    Teacher Resources **133**

    About the Editors **137**

Acknowledgments

We would like to express our appreciation and thanks to the members of our Editorial Advisory Board, Nancy Cloud, Jean Handscombe, and Ann Newton, who were instrumental in selecting the papers chosen for inclusion in this book. Their comments and suggestions were insightful and astute. We also thank Jack Richards, Chair of the TESOL Publications Committee, and the reviewers on the committee, whose guidance helped us shape this book.

In addition, Terry O'Donnell, TESOL Special Projects Coordinator; Helen Kornblum, TESOL Director of Communications and Marketing; Susan Bayley, TESOL Executive Director; and Ellen Garshick, Copy Editor, offered us valuable advice and guidance that facilitated the completion of the project. Finally, we acknowledge the TESOL Special Projects Grant that supported our work. Fred Genesee's leadership in initiating the Interest Section Special Projects helped this book see the light of day, and for that we are grateful.

1

Common Threads, Common Bonds

Denise McKeon
Katharine Davies Samway

"Teachers don't write." This unfortunate refrain has long been heard in academic circles. In fact, as we began this book, we, too, wondered if it was true. We knew that interest in teaching younger learners was growing but that teachers themselves had written very little about teaching English to speakers of other languages (ESOL) at the elementary level. We wished to address these omissions by compiling this book. A year and 40 submissions later, we are happy to report that teachers *do* write, and with a power and authenticity that make their stories compelling. The stories presented here provide glimpses of a type of teaching that has rarely been described in a comprehensive way: teaching ESOL in the primary grades (K–8) worldwide.[1]

We believe that this book reveals the variety of realities experienced by teachers of English around the world. You are likely, therefore, to find theoretical stances and instructional practices in one chapter that may seem at odds with those described in others. At the same time, you will find a remarkable degree of agreement across chapters, a level of common beliefs and practices that surface in extremely different contexts. This finding surprised and thrilled us as it reminded us of the common bonds that we share with teachers around the world.

Common Threads of Practice

When we examined the manuscripts that had been submitted, we noticed that certain *threads of practice* seemed to run through almost all of the descriptions of teaching ESOL. These common threads of practice lead

Common Threads of Practice

us to believe that, although those who teach ESOL to children frequently fail to have access to the exchange of ideas and camaraderie found in academic gatherings or professional development conferences, an overriding force shapes their teaching. We believe that force is the nature of children themselves.

The ESOL programs and classrooms described in this book, for example, are first and foremost *child-centered*. Although the theoretical and methodological approach may vary from place to place, the goal of each seems to be to provide language instruction that meets the cognitive, social, and emotional needs of children. Overwhelmingly, the instructional emphasis is on providing language experiences that are natural. We note a strong trend away from "drill and kill" activities that feature language used in a repetitious and highly structured way and, instead, a move toward language use that taps children's imagination and creativity: the use of children's literature, process writing, and language tied to content such as science or mathematics (see the chapters by Sherman and Stassen).

We have noticed, too, that language seems to be used in an integrated way. That is, there is an increased emphasis on teaching the four skills of language (listening, speaking, reading, and writing) as an integrated whole whose separate parts cannot be taught in isolation. We were struck by the degree to which reading and writing instruction has been incorporated into primary-level ESOL classes. However, this instruction revolves around children reading and writing for a real purpose: to enjoy a story, to learn about something, or to share their own original thoughts through writing. Children do not read specially written texts in which the grammar and story line are controlled to the detriment of a good story, but rather read (and are read) books that were written to be enjoyed by children (see the chapters by Rous, Eby, Stein, and Ng and Preston). Writing is not viewed as an opportunity to copy words or sentences selected for their semantic or grammatical usefulness. Instead, it is a meaning-making activity. The children select their topics and use writing to make sense of the world and to communicate their thoughts and feelings to others (see the chapters by Eby, Hoyt, Rous, Stassen, and Stein).

Just as they see language itself as an integrated whole, teachers are recognizing that first and second language development are also integrated. When the emphasis of a lesson is on meaning, teachers are more likely to incorporate the students' first language into the ESOL class as a bridge to understanding in English (see the chapters by Bi Qing, Hoyt, Ramahobo and Orr, and Poliak).

The variety of nontraditional staffing strategies employed by many

ESOL programs also attests to their attention to meaning. Evidence of team teaching, the use of peer assistants, and the presence of adults other than the ESOL teacher (such as parents or instructional assistants who speak the native language of the students) help to ensure that concepts presented through ESOL instruction are understood and reinforced (see the chapters by Bi Qing, Hoyt, Poliak, Syvanen, and Watson).

We also see ample evidence of attention to *children's social development* in ESOL classes. ESOL teachers worldwide are experimenting with new classroom structures such as cooperative or group learning and peer tutoring. Descriptions of group writing projects, small multilevel instructional groups, and an emphasis on topics that have meaning in the lives of the children contribute to our sense that teachers recognize that positive social growth is an important outcome of all instruction, including ESOL (see the chapters by Ng and Preston, Sherman, Stein, and Watson).

Social growth is tied almost inextricably to *student empowerment* and *the enhancement of student self-esteem* by ESOL teachers. Teachers show how they have taken great pains to structure learning environments that nurture children. Author after author relates with care and concern the need for children to feel good about learning and about themselves; examples of student triumphs, large and small, fill the pages of each article.

Particularly heartening are descriptions of everyday activities that seem remarkable given the context in which they occur: singing the nursery rhyme "Old MacDonald Had a Farm" in a Chinese kindergarten class, reading *The Three Billy Goats Gruff* (1987) in a second-grade class in Brunei Darussalam, and pretending to be Australian circus animals (who speak only English) in a Russian primary school. Perhaps most moving, however, are the stories that echo in the children's own writing: the effects of certain social, cultural, and political policies on children's lives. "The Lonely Hogan," written by a Navajo student in the United States (see the chapter by Eby), and "People Are Cross," written by a student in Soweto, South Africa (see the chapter by Stein), help to remind us that the lives and experiences of ESOL students, no matter how old, extend beyond the protection that a safe classroom context can provide.

Characteristics of ESOL Teachers

An additional theme that emerges from the stories told in this book concerns the characteristics of the ESOL professionals who design and provide instruction. Regardless of setting or constraints, the behavior of these professionals is characterized by what we term *conscientious practice*; that is, the thoughtful and reflective process of examining the impact of instruction on student learning. Although the instructional practices described in each of the articles show evidence of being dynamic and evolving, teachers are attending to the relationship between theoretical models of instruction and the performance of students in their classes. They are firsthand observers of what works and what doesn't. They are researchers of the first order: designing hypotheses of what will work in a given context, trying them out, and examining the results.

Above all, the stories in this book paint a portrait of ESOL teachers as concerned professionals who put children first. They go to great lengths to design and carry out instruction that will leave children with a love of learning. They create excitement and fun in their classes, harness the power of student imagination, and actively involve students as partners in the enterprise of education.

The Sociopolitical Context of Language Teaching

The forces that impel even very young children to study and learn English are quite varied; the sociopolitical context in which English is taught emerges as the final theme running through each of the chapters in this book. In a great many parts of the world, English is highly regarded and, particularly in countries or contexts where it is not a dominant language, knowledge of English is interconnected with social class and power. Multilingualism is prized in these contexts, and English often occupies a key role in one's language repertoire (see the chapter by Felberbauer). For some children in these situations, learning English is a logical extension of their privileged position in the world and their extensive experience with formal education. For example, many of the native German-speaking children in the German School Washington (see the chapter by Stassen) are learning English as a second, third, or fourth language. Their native language, German, is highly respected, and much of their education continues to be conducted in German. Students not only are learning English but are becoming bilingual and biliterate (if not trilingual and triliterate) citizens of a global village.

In contrast, children learning English in Soweto, South Africa (see the chapter by Stein), are doing so because all formal education beyond age 10 is conducted in English. The native languages of Black South

African children are not recognized by the school system. Although English is spoken as a native language by a minority of South Africans, it enjoys a privileged position, and young Black South Africans must, against heavy odds, become adept in English if they are to take advantage of the few educational and economic opportunities available to them.

In other, equally troubling cases, particularly in countries that have large language minority populations and where English is the dominant language, such as the United States, English is not only a gatekeeper to academic survival and advancement; it may be seen as a replacement for, rather than an addition to, the child's first language. Except for a relatively small number of language programs that seek to strengthen and maintain the child's first language while teaching English, the value of bilingualism for these students is largely repudiated.

The diverse sociopolitical contexts of English language teaching result in some strange dualities. Language can free or oppress, replace or add to, enrich or impoverish. These facts make one thing clear: Understanding the sociopolitical context in which English is learned is as integral to good language teaching as understanding the nature of second language learning.

Conclusion

In many cases we do not know if the classrooms and programs portrayed here are representative of official educational practice throughout the various countries described. Nevertheless, we offer these glimpses of teaching ESOL to children around the world as examples of current instructional practice from which all of us can learn.[2] As educators learn more about the practice of teaching ESOL worldwide, the dynamism and evolution of theory and practice can continue to flourish.

Notes

1. The term ESOL includes all children learning English as a nonnative language: in countries where English is the dominant, common language (e.g., the United States), where English is one of two or more official languages (e.g., Brunei Darussalam), and where English is not an official or dominant language (e.g., Austria or China). These differences in the status of and need for English are reflected in the degree to which children encounter English in their everyday lives and in the immediate need (or motivation) for them to know English.

2. We had hoped to include manuscripts from a variety of English-speaking countries and all continents. Regrettably, we failed to receive any submissions from Canada, Great Britain, Australia, or South America.

References

The three billy goats gruff. (1987). New York: Scholastic/TAB Publications.

2

For a Brighter Future
SPEAK Project in Soweto

Pippa Stein

In 1985, Pippa Stein and Martha Mokgoko started SPEAK, a privately funded English language teaching project for children in Soweto, South Africa. Stein states that the original aim of SPEAK was to help children "find their voices." In this chapter she describes the genesis of SPEAK within the Soweto educational context and focuses on the English language teaching approach used in the project. She outlines the materials and activities that worked with learners and includes pieces of student writing that illustrate the power of the project.

Stein is a member of the Department of Applied English Language Studies, University of the Witwatersrand, Johannesburg, South Africa.

Soweto is a high-density Black ghetto on the outskirts of Johannesburg where the majority of the people speak English as a second or third language. Although the majority of Sowetans have an African language as their mother tongue, English is widely perceived as an international language providing access to the worlds of business and education. Whatever language policies a future government makes, English is likely to remain an important language of access.

English is the language of education in Soweto. For the first 4 years of school Black children learn through the medium of their mother tongue and study English as a school subject. In the fifth year of schooling, at the approximate age of 10,[1] there is an abrupt switch from mother-tongue instruction to English as the medium of instruction. This transition causes serious cognitive and linguistic difficulties for the children, who often can barely read and write English.[2]

Martha Mokgoko and I have been working together since 1982 as teacher trainers in a programme for Soweto higher primary school teachers to assist them in helping children make the transition from mother-tongue instruction to English in the Standard 3 year.[3] This programme aimed to improve the teachers' general teaching skills, with a focus on English language teaching (ELT), by trying to introduce a more learner-centred methodology into the classroom.[4]

The task was a very difficult one. We became increasingly frustrated at our lack of progress in changing teachers' attitudes from a transmission style to an interactive model of teaching English. Most Soweto teachers are products of Bantu Education, a system that encourages a top-down, transmission model of teaching that is antithetical to critical thinking. Teachers expect learners not to question knowledge but to produce "the right answer." Teachers are thus afraid to broach controversial subjects, and students are reluctant to enter into discussion for fear of not agreeing with the teacher.

In addition, teachers have to work in overcrowded classrooms (an average of 40–50 children) with a lack of resources: insufficient textbooks and class readers, no electricity, and few school libraries. A transmission style of teaching is less demanding for a teacher under these conditions.

We were also concerned about the practice of ELT at the higher primary school level, which was usually based on a formal or structural syllabus. Teachers relied heavily on the prescribed grammar textbooks, which left little opportunity for communicative language use. Teachers insisted that students produce grammatically correct sentences whenever they spoke English. The idea that errors might be evidence of language learning was foreign. As a result, children were afraid to speak English for fear of making mistakes and being punished.

The teaching of reading consisted for the most part of groups or individuals reading aloud from the prescribed classroom readers, which students found boring and unattractive. These readers bore little relationship to the children's interests or realities.[5] Teachers paid no attention to developing children's reading strategies in a second language. Very few schools had school or class libraries, so reading for pleasure was, for the majority of children, an alien practice.

The teaching of writing was product oriented. The teacher always set the topic and prepared children with vocabulary and structures in a form of guided writing. Topics such as *My School* or *An Accident I Witnessed* were typical. Students did no free writing.

ELT in the average Soweto Standard 3 classroom showed little understanding of the processes involved in the development of English as a second language (ESL) communicative skills. The establishment in most classes of a teacher-led pattern of communication left no room for spontaneous, exploratory talk through pair or group work, free discussion, or learner-initiated talk. Children were not given opportunities to engage in genuine meaning-making language activities.

The Need for Change

Macdonald (1990) has argued that, when the teacher talks all the time and the pupils talk only in tightly constrained instances, children are prevented from developing generative language skills and their language production remains largely imitative. Children in Soweto were not being exposed to the full range of language functions identified by Halliday (1975) for general language use, which was seriously impeding genuine learning at the conceptual level.

Teachers were also operating under external constraints that impinged on classroom practice. Apartheid education was authoritarian and oppressive. Syllabi set by state educational authorities had to be rigidly adhered to, education authorities regularly inspected schools, and certain topics—sex, politics, and religion—were banned from the classroom. Teachers had very little freedom within their own classrooms.

Martha and I found it increasingly oppressive to work within the confines of this educational context. We believed we could find another way of working with children and teachers, but it had to be outside the state system, using private funding, where we could work in a free and open atmosphere.

SPEAK classes started in July 1985 with funds donated by a leading mining house for a 3-month pilot programme. In view of the serious language difficulties experienced by Standard 3 children in making the switch from mother tongue to English as the medium of instruction, we decided to begin working with Standard 3 children only. We enrolled 100 volunteer students from local schools to attend after-school classes for 1 1/2 hours once a week at Ipelegeng Centre, the local community centre.

Two guiding principles established at the start formed the core of our language teaching and learning approach in SPEAK. Our success in empowering teachers and students has depended a great deal on them. First, we believed that if we could offer children a learning experience in English that had as its guiding principle a *genuine search for meaning*, we could effect change on a number of levels:

─────────── **Common Threads of Practice** ───────────

- the children's ESL communicative competence would increase
- their self-confidence and sense of self-worth would develop
- their critical thinking skills could be developed through engagement with meaningful content.

Second, we wanted to create an atmosphere of freedom and learner responsibility in the classroom. In such an environment no topics for discussion were taboo. Children had to learn to listen to each other and respect each other's rights to different opinions. Teachers had to learn to listen to and respect the opinions of the children. This mutual respect is very hard to engender in South Africa, where there is no tradition of religious, racial, or political tolerance.

Our decision to concentrate on developing self-confidence on a personal and linguistic level led us to work within an acquisition model of language teaching. The overemphasis in state schools on the production of grammatically correct sentences had instilled in the children a fear of speaking English. We countered this fear by introducing fluency activities and by encouraging children to speak freely in an atmosphere where error was tolerated. Because Martha and I had been concerned at the lack of praise and encouragement in many Soweto classrooms, SPEAK teachers were encouraged to provide regular positive feedback to children to develop their sense of self-worth and lower their affective filters.

From the outset Martha and I were working in isolation. At times we felt we were working in the dark, as there were no similar models in the country against which we could measure ourselves. In addition, the social and political conditions under which we were attempting to establish SPEAK were very difficult. Our first classes began the same week that the apartheid government declared a national state of emergency. Troops patrolled Soweto continuously, and the army invaded schools. Many high school students were detained; some were shot. It was a period of mass struggle, boycotts, and defiance campaigns.

On several occasions it was too dangerous for the teaching staff and children to attend classes. A SPEAK report from that time states:

> The atmosphere of violence and brutality has had a deep emotional effect on the community. There have been times when the children have come to classes so distressed and shocked at what was happening that the SPEAK teachers were unable to carry out their intended lesson plans and simply played games to help calm the children down. (Stein, 1985)

In spite of these conditions, the children continued to come to classes.

The SPEAK Programme

Our projected syllabus plan for the first year consisted of a beginner's course focusing on useful functions needed by the children, such as greeting others, buying items in a shop, and asking for directions. The focus was on developing oral skills. Although SPEAK children had been learning English at school as a subject for 4 years, they needed opportunities to practise speaking English spontaneously for social use. We developed an extended picture story showing a typical Soweto family shopping in the centre of Johannesburg on a Saturday morning (Figure 1). The pictures caused quite a stir amongst the children, who had not seen pictures of their own environment in ELT textbooks before.

Although we had initially planned to concentrate only on developing oral skills in the first year, we quickly realised that separating the skills was a mistake. We therefore decided to introduce a writing component, using the children's daily experiences as the topics for talking and writing. Every week we set aside some time for exploratory talk and free writing on issues of concern to the children. This regular feature of SPEAK was called "Behind the Headlines." The title was fitting: At the time, the media were severely restricted by the emergency regulations, and any reports of unrest in Soweto were heavily censored.

The pieces of free writing in Figures 2, 3, and 4 were written in 1986 by individual or groups of SPEAK children. They describe events such as the bus boycott, the school boycotts, and consumer boycotts taking place in Soweto at that time. The name *comrade* is the colloquial name given to members of the African National Congress (ANC) and its aligned political movements. "In Soweto Today" (Figure 2) refers to the bus boycott, and "People Are Cross" (Figure 3) refers to the school boycotts and the ongoing battles between the apartheid police and Soweto schoolchildren, many of whom were shot by police in 1976. In "We Suggest" (Figure 4), the writers describe a notorious incident during a consumer boycott, when a Soweto woman broke the boycott by buying groceries from White-owned shops in the centre of Johannesburg.

Part of our work in SPEAK was to help children to reflect critically on the social and material conditions of their lives so they could understand the root causes of the violence they were witnessing. We wanted to promote a culture of talking rather than of fighting. One of the ways we did this successfully was through drama.

In 1988, Martha worked with the class to create an original play with a Standard 4 class called *Mishak's Bicycle*, based on one child's experience in Soweto. Mishak was a 12-year-old boy whose father had

Common Threads of Practice

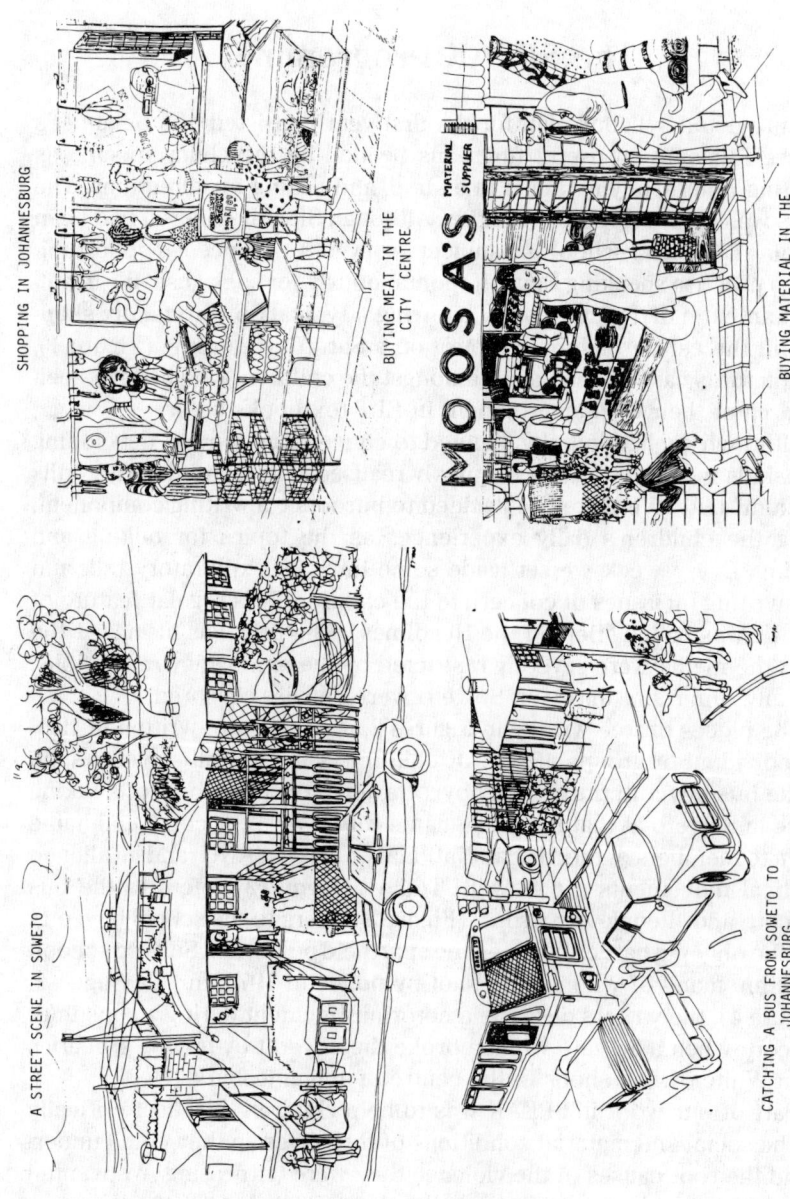

Figure 1. Picture story for speaking practice.

In Soweto Today

In Soweto there are many groups, like the comrades, who are saying, "We want freedom." The whites are killing the blacks, the blacks are killing other blacks. That's why we say, "Black against black," but it must be black against white.

At home my parents are not happy because they can't go to work for their children. If our parents are on a bus, the school children come in and tell them to get out before they burn the bus. And the driver has to run away. Our parents are struggling with transport.

At church our priest is praying for freedom. Other people are praying for people to live in peace. Sometimes our priest makes a special day to pray for Afrika. On that day we pray at the Regina Mundi Church and we don't want hippos[1] but they come.

Figure 2. Free writing on the Soweto bus boycott. [1]Hippos are large army vehicles that look like hippopotamuses. They are used extensively to patrol the Black townships.

People Are Cross
Samuel Dambuza (Age 12)

People are cross because the police are throwing teargas and chasing us out of our schools. The big meetings of the pupils are held in the Regina Mundi Church. If there is a meeting there, all the people of power must be there. Then the shops are closed and we get hungry.

The comrades have chased us out of our schools. Some of the children are happy because they don't want to go to school and write examinations. But me, I want to write examinations because I want to be clever.

At church they are praying for us to live in peace in Soweto and for the pupils who are dying—for those who died in 1976[1] and for those who have no legs.

Figure 3. Free writing on school boycotts and police-student conflicts in Soweto. [1]Many schoolchildren were shot by police in the Soweto uprisings in 1976.

Common Threads of Practice

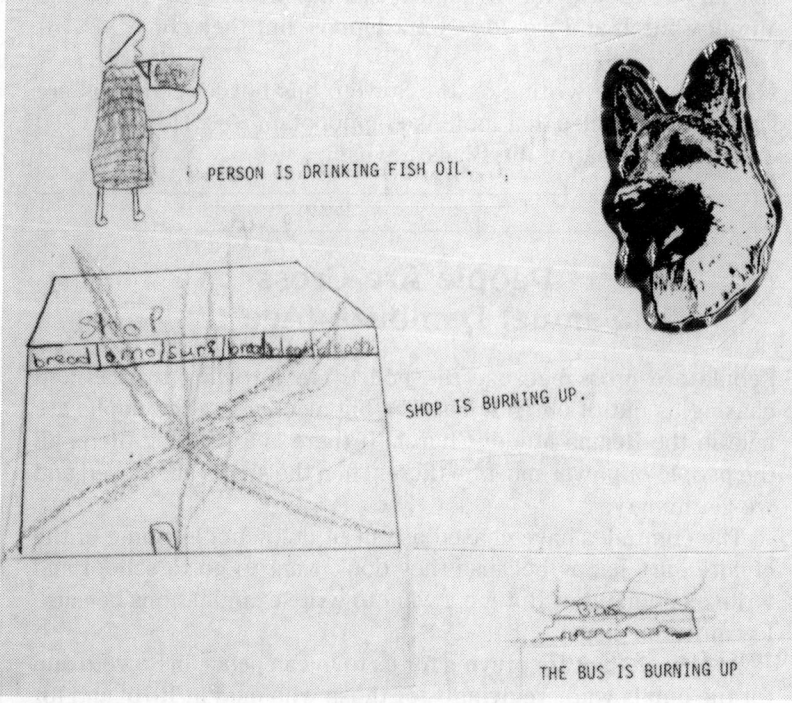

WE SUGGEST

In this picture the woman is drinking fish oil. The shops are burning. We see dogs and a burning bus. People are not supposed to drink fish oil because they will get a disease. It seems that this woman was forced to drink fish oil because when the comrades said we must not buy in town she became stubborn and bought groceries in town. It is very clear that if people drink fish oil they will suffer and die. We suggest that people must not burn shops and buses because we cannot travel easily. We suggest that we must not burn shops because we need food. We cannot live without food.

Busiswe, Jeremiah, Nonhlanhla, Thumeka and Innocentia.

PERSON IS DRINKING FISH OIL.

SHOP IS BURNING UP.

THE BUS IS BURNING UP

Figure 4. Free writing on the consumer boycott in Soweto.

For a Brighter Future

saved up to buy him a bicycle for his birthday. One afternoon, three thieves robbed Mishak of his bicycle at gunpoint. Mishak's older brother went looking for the thieves. He found one of them and, with Mishak's father's help, beat him up. They then took the thief to the police, who subsequently released him without charges. Mishak never reclaimed his bicycle. The play ended with a poem written by the class, pleading for joint community action against the high levels of crime in Soweto. Apartheid was cited as the prime cause of this violence.

Martha has commented on the process of making this play:

> At the time, the children were undergoing political strain. It was tense in the class. I decided that we should talk about the daily events and as we talked, many stories emerged. As we discussed these stories, the children began to relax. For some problems, they didn't have solutions but through discussion, we came up with solutions. We laughed too, about very serious things.
>
> We heard each other's stories and we negotiated which one to use for the play. It was painful ... you found there was agreement and disagreement amongst the children but we wanted to encourage debate, not fighting. We then had a series of workshops on Mishak's story to make the script. The whole process was very communicative. For example, in order to find the thief, Mishak's brother had to give him a perfect description of him. For this scene we gave each child in the class an opportunity to describe the thief in a creative way. Mishak would then decide if the description was true. This became very comic.
>
> The children learnt a lot from this process. They learnt how to observe carefully, how to investigate, what kinds of questions to ask a thief. ... It also gave them a chance to reflect on the situation. This person was beaten up, but we don't encourage this kind of violence. At the end of the day, you are building the children, you are educating the whole person for the future. These children are our future leaders. Next time Mishak meets a problem like this, he will say, halt. We must act collectively and the violence will stop. We are asking people to think, not just to use their feelings. We also want them to be creative in English—to make a play and write a poem from this experience.

Mishak's Bicycle was performed at the SPEAK Children's Day for children and parents, an annual cultural event in which teachers and children present poems, stories, and original plays for parents and the local community. At the end of the performance, Mishak's father thanked the project for giving his son the opportunity to reenact this traumatic experience for the community to witness. "What you have seen today," he said, "is how apartheid has turned a law-abiding, respectable fellow like myself into a thug."

Common Threads of Practice

At a certain point we consulted with the children on what they would like to talk and read about in SPEAK classes. A recurring request was for "our hidden history," that is, the history of Black people in South Africa from a Black point of view. In state schools, South African history is told from a White point of view. Much of the history of Black communities and their struggle for liberation is omitted from history textbooks, so students end up with a very distorted sense of history.

We responded to this request by developing two courses on the hidden history: *The Sophiatown Removals*, a task-based workbook about a multiracial freehold suburb called Sophiatown that was destroyed by the apartheid state in the 1950s and declared a Whites-only suburb, and the Oral History Project, a learner-led project that focused on writing up the histories of the SPEAK children's families and communities. Both of these courses were developed for Standard 5 children, who were older than the Standard 3 children (12–15 years old) and more ready to engage with the intellectual demands of exploring history.

The Sophiatown Removals workbook contains a wide range of tasks drawing on students' linguistic, cognitive, and visual literacy skills. Students are required to describe and analyse photographs from the period, to read personal accounts of how people lived at the time, to interview their neighbours and community members who lived in Sophiatown, and to write up their stories. Discussion and critical reflection on why the apartheid state forcibly removed people from Sophiatown to a Black-only residential area called Meadowlands are an integral part of this process and feed into a larger discussion on why Black people in South Africa have been forcibly relocated throughout colonial history. The workbook includes a literature component with poems, songs, and stories about Sophiatown, which was famous for its cultural life.

The Oral History Project grew out of the Sophiatown project. In the course of finding out about whether their parents knew or lived in Sophiatown, students started getting interested in their own family histories. In the Oral History Project, students researched their own history, then published it in a book called *My Own History Book*. The purpose of the project was to give students a sense of the value of their own histories. In contrast to school history books, which present the view that history is made by great men and women, we wanted to focus on the role ordinary people play in the shaping of history.

The first task in the Oral History Project workbook, a discussion on "What is History?", sparked heated debate amongst teachers and children, who said, "We don't want to learn about Jan Van Riebeeck. We are sick of learning about White history. We want to learn about the history of Black people." Some teachers responded by saying, "We need to know

For a Brighter Future

White history to understand our oppression." The SPEAK project aims were the deciding factor. If Blacks and Whites were to work together to reconcile our differences, we needed to come out of the process of reconstruction as one nation. This meant that we needed to research and critically evaluate both perspectives.

These history courses brought to the surface a lot of the children's anger about the effects of apartheid on their families' lives. One child's great-grandfather refused to be interviewed because he did not want to recall the bitterness of the past. Teachers felt that they could use the Oral History Project as one way of dealing with that anger.

Using a process syllabus model, teachers and children jointly decided how to go about constructing the project. Teachers found this process of syllabus design rather daunting, as each week brought new surprises. The teachers were initially quite surprised at the children's response to the discussion on history and quite unprepared for the parents' response to the children's questions about the family history. One parent complained that her daughter was asking too many questions and that she did not know how to answer them: "I don't want to tell my daughter the family secrets," she said. We had to call a parents' meeting to resolve the issue. Some parents complained that their children were asking them about the family tree, and in some cases, in which the children concerned were illegitimate, parents were reluctant to disclose the name of the father or mother. After lengthy debate on this issue, the parents concluded that the project was educationally sound and supported it.

The following excerpt is from *My Own History Book*, by Thabo Makoko, aged 11.

The Story of My Grandfather, John

My name is John. I was born in 1932 at Maputo Village. Then in 1936 I went to Botswana and in 1940 I went to Lesotho. Then in 1946 I went to Lebowa. The reason that I went to these places is that there were no streams for us to quench our thirst and the houses were too small for us to live in so we were looking for a bigger house.

In Lebowa I went to school for eight years then I left school to become a doctor. At school we wore uniforms, black trousers and white shirts.

When I was young life was fine but there was no food, no money and no clothes. Our parents were very poor so we suffered a lot. We worked so hard to get money to buy clothes, food, shoes and to pay rent.

In our country there were many fights and they were all about peace. This peace meant that people wanted to live like white people.

I came here to Soweto because I thought life would be better and food would be easy to get. Because work was all over and we worked hard and we got so much money.

Conclusion

SPEAK is now 6 years old. The future of the project is uncertain, as private funding is becoming more and more difficult to obtain. There are two centres in Soweto catering to the needs of 400 children. Eleven Soweto primary school teachers have been trained to teach part time on the project. Martha Mokgoko is establishing a new SPEAK centre in Alexandra, a Black residential area in Johannesburg. I am an ELT consultant to the project.

Martha and I started SPEAK because we believed children learning ESL in Soweto primary schools deserved a better educational deal. The ELT approach outlined above has come about in direct response to a specific context and the needs of the learner group in this context. Our primary aim was to help children to find their voices. Through the use of issue-driven teaching materials and activities that break down fear, encourage debate, and involve the students in using language to make their own meanings, we have witnessed motivation levels increase dramatically. Students become interested in learning English when they have a personal investment in the issues under discussion.

Working predominantly within a fluency model has paid off well. SPEAK children speak English with confidence and without shame because they feel safe from criticism. They become creative with language because they come to understand the power of language. English is no longer the inaccessible language of the colonial oppressor—it is *their* language to use for their own purposes.

Notes

1. Education for Black children is not compulsory, as it is for White children. As a result, children may start school late or drop out and then return to school the following year. Often there are children in Standard 3 who are 12 or 13 years old.
2. For a detailed account of the controversy over medium of instruction in South African education, see Janks (1990). For more background on the difficulties encountered by students in making the switch from mother-tongue instruction to English, see Macdonald (1990).
3. Primary schools in Soweto are divided into lower and higher primary levels. The lower level consists of the first 4 years of formal schooling, known as Sub A, Sub B, Standard 1, and Standard 2. The higher level consists of the 5th, 6th, and 7th years of schooling, known as Standards 3, 4, and 5. The SPEAK project works with children from the higher primary level.

4. This programme, called the Schools' English Language Research Project, was run from the University of Witwatersrand, Johannesburg. It was one of the few programmes of its kind that was given permission from the state education system (the Department of Education and Training) to work in state schools.
5. In many schools there are insufficient numbers of class readers for all the students. Even though the readers are tiresome, they are all the students have to read at the moment.

References

Halliday, M. A. K. (1975). *Learning how to mean: Explorations in the development of language.* London: Edward Arnold.

Janks, H. (1990). Contested terrain: English education in South Africa. In I. Goodson & P. Medway (Eds.), *Bringing English to order: The history and politics of a school subject.* Lewes, East Sussex, England: Falmer Press.

Macdonald, C. A. (1990). *English language skills evaluation* (Final report of the Threshold Project). Pretoria: Human Sciences Research Council.

Stein, P. (1985). *SPEAK project report.* Johannesburg.

3

The "Essence of Sliding"

Encouraging Elementary ESL Students to Become Creative Writers

J. Wesley Eby

More than 500 Native American students attend Wingate Elementary School near Gallup, New Mexico, a boarding school operated by the Bureau of Indian Affairs of the U.S. government for children in Grades K–8. Navajo is the first language for 80% of the students.

J. Wesley Eby, who worked for many years as a teacher-administrator at Wingate, discusses the comprehensive language program used there. He describes several key activities that facilitated the development of the children's reading and writing skills and illustrates the results of the program in several vivid examples of student work.

One frigid, wintry morning I visited an eighth-grade language arts class and watched while the teacher skillfully set the stage for a creative writing assignment about the month of February. The students began the task immediately and industriously. Later, when the teacher shared the students' drafts with me, one brief composition caught my attention. I looked at it again and again. It was written by a Navajo English as a second language (ESL) learner, drafted quickly on a sheet of white notebook paper by a likable, capable chap:

Sliding
The essence of sliding is to be careful and enjoy it at the same time. Sliding can be real fun when you share it with someone. You can laugh

The Essence of Sliding

and be scared when you go down a hill on a sled. The idea to winter is to have fun with it while you have the chance.

> Winter
>
> People filled with chills,
>   Their body crested against the cold air.
> People celebrating the new year
>   by sliding.
> A way to make the snow useful.

As I read the words, "Their body crested against the cold air," I shivered. I realized, however, that my body reacted not just to the icy image he created with a few, succinct words but to the emotion and excitement I felt from reading a powerful piece of writing.

Then I thought of other days, other classes, other teachers, other students. This piece was just one of countless original writings I had read during 3 years at the school. They were penned not by children from a socioeconomically advantaged suburb of Phoenix, Arizona, or Albuquerque, New Mexico, but by Navajo students who lived on or near the Navajo Reservation in northern New Mexico and Arizona.

Student Population

Wingate Elementary School near Gallup, New Mexico, is a boarding school operated by the U.S. Bureau of Indian Affairs for children in Grades K–8. Over 90% of the more than 500 Native American students live in dormitories. The school often enrolls students who have dropped out of public schools. Navajo is the first language of 80% of the students. They have grown up in a culture that does not have a written literature, and printed material of any kind in their first language is greatly limited. Many of the students have health problems, especially visual impairments, that often hamper their learning and academic success.

On a typical day, boarding school students are awakened at 6:00 a.m. by their Navajo dormitory parents. The time before classes is used for getting ready, eating breakfast in the school cafeteria, and performing housekeeping chores, such as making beds and cleaning their own living areas. After lunch, while the teachers have a break, the students return to their dormitories for recreation, Indian Club activities, or free time. Students attend classes for 6 hours a day. After classes are dismissed in the afternoon, most students have free time. Many of the older students are involved in organized sports. After dinner Monday through Thursday, all students are required to participate in a 1-hour study period. Evenings are also used for shopping trips to nearby Gallup or to attend ball games, movies, or concerts. Students can also choose to participate in a variety of clubs or activities. Bedtime is 9:00 p.m. for the younger children and an hour later for the older students.

Most students go home for the weekends. Parents or relatives arrive at the school by mid-afternoon on Fridays to pick up their children, returning with them on Sunday evening. A few students are able to go home only once a month. For these children, the dorm parents and recreation staff provide a wide range of activities on the weekends, from nature hikes and picnics to trips to the Navajo museum and Indian powwows.

The Curriculum

How did Wingate students become creative writers? Such writing had not always been the norm at Wingate or in the other schools on the Navajo Reservation, where I worked for almost two decades. The academic staff labored diligently and conscientiously at teaching ESL. Although we saw improvement in the students' language, their English production was not what we desired, lacking in both quantity and quality. Their low scores on standardized achievement tests, which were required by government regulations, disheartened us.

Finally, the Wingate administration decided to make a drastic change: to overhaul the curriculum and implement a whole language approach. Moving away from DISTAR, a behavioristic, stimulus-response program then in use, was a big step, but Wingate's administrative team agreed to try whole language and to introduce it to teachers and students alike in a summer school workshop of 3 weeks and 2 days.

How, then, were we able to get "the essence of sliding" from our students? We simply established two goals:

1. to bring the world to the children and to take the children into the world
2. to create a rich language environment for the students by integrating reading and writing across the curriculum.

The environment created by these goals encouraged the students to take risks, to explore, to create; we were concerned more that students express meaning and content than that they use correct language forms.

─────────────── **The Essence of Sliding** ───────────────

We accomplished our goals by using the nine key activities described below. None of them is new; all have been around for years. We simply expanded them and sometimes gave them a different or special "twist"—the Wingate way.

Reading Aloud to the Students

Students and teachers engaged in this tried-and-tested activity several times a day: in departmentalized and content area classes, in special education resource rooms (designed to provide special assistance to physically or mentally challenged youngsters), in Chapter I labs (set up to assist students struggling with basic skills such as reading and math), and in the dormitories at night. Reading aloud was a required activity for all teachers and staff members.

Reading materials consisted of library books, other trade books, magazines, newspapers, content area books, and student-authored stories. This activity, a beginning point, epitomized what we were striving to accomplish throughout the program: to create a rich language environment through reading across the curriculum and bringing the world to the children.

SSR: Sustained, Silent Reading

SSR was required in all classes and dormitories. We wanted the children to realize that reading was more than an academic activity—that it was a lifelong pursuit. We also believed that the students could and should exert control over most of their own reading.

To keep the SSR concept motivating and challenging, we implemented WKRP, or Wingate Karate Reading Program. We wanted the students to begin reading materials they had selected themselves from literature other than comic books and magazines. The WKRP Committee developed extensive book lists, and the students were required to select at least two thirds of their books from the approved lists. When the students read a particular number of books, they were awarded karate belts—long colorful ribbons with the school mascot, a bear cub, reading a book. The white belt was earned after reading 10 books. Each belt added 10 or more books. The black belt required a total of 225 books, certainly not a 1-year program. The WKRP reading record became a part of the students' cumulative folders.

Another Wingate twist to the SSR concept was called Million Minutes. It started with a challenge by the principal to the students: "I bet you can't read a million minutes this year!" The students accepted the wager and began to read. Because 90% of the students lived in school dormitories, SSR was added to the dormitory study hour four nights a week. The dorm parents maintained records, and progress was graphically charted on the school's cafeteria ceiling each week. The challenge was issued in early November; the students passed the million mark in May.

When asked to determine what would happen to the principal when the students won the bet, the creative leaders on the student council decided they would like the principal and all staff members to come to school dressed as punk rockers for a day. The staff cooperated, giving the students a memorable day by showing up in everything from black leather and pink hair to wrist spikes.

For our students, SSR was not simply an activity tossed into the schedule if there was time. We believed that children become proficient readers through ample, meaningful practice. SSR was an important way for the students to acquire that needed practice, and it immersed them in a rich language environment that brought the world to them through the printed page.

Literature Studies

Teachers were encouraged to begin in-depth reading instruction in trade books. Basal readers were not discarded, but teachers were given permission to substitute literature studies for more traditional reading programs.

One memorable literature study about King Arthur was conducted by the two language arts teachers in the middle school. The students discussed the novel extensively. In addition, they built a castle out of sugar cubes and constructed a mail coat of armor. At the end of the 3-week study, the novel served as the theme for the eighth-grade banquet and graduation; the school cafeteria was transformed into Camelot. King Arthur was indelibly etched in the reading memories of these middle school students.

Thematic Units

We began to teach in thematic units to ensure that reading and writing would be more effectively integrated across the curriculum. For example, one sixth-grade teacher planned a unit on newspapers each year. The students wrote one or more letters to various cities, requesting newspapers for a designated date. The response was overwhelming. Students were elated as they received newspapers in different languages, letters, and chamber-of-commerce materials from around the world.

─────────────── **The Essence of Sliding** ───────────────

Reading and writing took on new meaning as students encountered social studies, science, and math concepts in new and interesting contexts. One year a Boston newspaper called the school and interviewed three students for an article. Later the lucky three were able to read the article written by the reporter (an exciting experience for any young student), which came about as the result of a letter requesting a newspaper.

For one thematic unit, all the teachers in Grades 7 and 8 (language arts, math, science, social studies, music, art, physical education, industrial arts, home economics, special education, and Chapter I lab) worked together to create a unit on survival. The academic staff met to brainstorm and plan what each member would do. Over a 4-week period, the students were immersed in the concept of survival in each class. Science tied survival to the environment; home economics linked survival to Navajo foods before Whites and trading posts came to the reservation; industrial arts dealt with survival and the use of hand tools. The math teacher helped the students compare the cost of living off the land with that of living in a consumer-driven economy. The art teacher had the students make and fire their own pottery as the early Navajos did to survive. Reading and writing across the curriculum also offered opportunities to reinforce literacy skills in a variety of contexts.

Journals

Keeping student journals, a familiar activity in many ESL classes today, helped many nonwriting students make the transition to writing. One of the most commonly used journal activities at all levels is the dialogue or response journal. A problem for teachers, though, is finding time to respond to the students, especially in departmentalized classes where teachers may have 120 or more students per day. Wingate's middle school solved this problem by scheduling time for response journals during the homeroom period. Every staff member, including the building principal, took a homeroom group. Because there were only 7–10 students per homeroom, responding daily to each student's journal became easier.

The use of journals was successfully extended by several non–language arts teachers. These content journals provided an opportunity for students to record their reactions to and feelings about the content they were being taught and to summarize their learning for the day. The following journal entries from one second grader illustrate how journal activities helped in the development of writing fluency:

―――――― **Common Threads of Practice** ――――――

September 18 (the day the journal began)
   I like to go to school. I do not my sister and my borther.

September (undated, but probably the next day)
   I like my litter borther and I like my mom and like my bike me

March 19 (same school year, 6 months later)
   I like to play when it is spring. I go to town when It is spring my friend like to play with me at home. They be nice to me. When It is spring I will go to town with my father and my mother, too. My friend like to play with me ih the spring. I like spring it makes me happy. My friend likes spring too.
   Me and my brother like spring. we be nice to our mather and our father. My friend like to play when It is spring. We play out side when it is spring. I like to carry lambs with my brother. My friends like to carry lambs too. we feed our lambs we give milk to them. We let them stay in our house. They get warm I feed them.

The author of these entries struggled with writing when the teacher first started the journal process but began to develop writing fluency through the journal activities conducted each day.

Process Writing

Process writing, or writing workshop, helped our students become creative writers. Once the children learned that they were experts on certain topics and really did have something to say, creativity was a cinch. Students drafted, and drafted, and drafted; revised, and revised, and revised; edited and edited; then published. As teachers and aides conferred with the students throughout all the stages of the process, rough drafts became polished compositions.
   In late August, at the beginning of the school year, a third grader wrote the following story:

My Horse

   My horse is brown. My horse can run fast. P. O. is wild. And it has a friend. His name is Big Red. The horses are P. O. and Big Red. Big Red is brown too. They can run fast. Big Red is lazy like me. My dog helps us chase the horses back. I have seven horses at home.

In February, just 6 months later, the same student wrote:

The Essence of Sliding

The Black Horse

Once upon a time there was a horse. It was black. It ran fast. I took a picture of him. I showed my boss the picture of the horse. My boss said, "Bring me the horse." I went back to get the horse but he was gone. He was running around the barn. I ran to him. I jumped on him. He took off running real fast.

I took him to a race. The man shouted, "Go." We took off. We came in first place. We got a prize. The prize was a trophy. We went back home and I fed him hay.

I will call him Black Stallion. I made a suit for me. The suit was black. People called me Zorro. I got a sword. I got on Black Stallion and we rode off to the east. We saved the people.

Someone hit the king. The king was dead. We started home. Someone threw an arrow at me. It hit me and I fell off the horse. The Black Stallion kicked the man. The man was dead. The Black Stallion was sad. He was lonely. He said, "I wish Zorro was here." He took off real fast to the west. Nobody saw Zorro or the Black Stallion again.

What a marked change! We quickly realized that promoting daily student writing resulted in remarkable progress in language production.

Sharing—an important part of writing journals—was even more so in process writing. Anxious to share their compositions, children clamored to be first and enthusiastically read their drafts and finished stories. Process writing encouraged many students to write, and some became prolific authors. Through process writing and journals, nonwriters became writers and nonreaders became readers. As never before in my 29 years in elementary education, I saw the interrelatedness of reading and writing.

Special Days

The special days that Wingate celebrated regularly throughout the year provided an opportunity to plan instructional activities that tied meaningful language to holidays, special events, and everyday life.

For example, backwardness invaded every area of the school and curriculum on Backwards Day. The school schedule was reversed, the cafeteria served dinner for breakfast and vice versa, and the staff and students wore their clothes backwards. But this special day was much more than a crazy, enjoyable time. It helped the students make some important discoveries about sequencing. One teacher read a story backwards to see if the students could understand it. The home economics teacher had the students follow a recipe in reverse to have them observe the tragic results firsthand. Science experiments done out of sequence helped the students learn why directions need to be followed carefully. Backwards Day proved to be a real eye-opener for the students.

During American Indian Week, the school was transformed into a Navajo fair. In addition to the classroom activities, the students and staff wore Native American ceremonial dress and participated in powwows, Indian dances, and fried bread contests. One year a large tepee was erected in the middle of the campus. Because special days helped to focus student attention on a specific topic, powerful student writing often emerged, as seen in this poem composed during American Indian Week:

> Grandfather
>
> A man of great wisdom
> looks me in the eye,
> tells me of a great,
> powerful spirit.
>
> The spirit of mankind
>
> As he speaks on to me,
> the words shock me,
> like electrical waves conquering the mind.
> All of sudden we're in a cloudland of beauty,
> on an open field.
>
> As he speaks on,
> we land where we began.
>
> Now he is like an open book of history
> for the whole world to read.

Artists-in-Residence Program

The artists-in-residence program brought the world to our students in a special way. It exposed them to a wide range of arts and other cultural experiences. During a 4-year span, 27 artists of all kinds visited the school for periods from 3 days to 9 months. These included

- two Native American poets and musicians
- a woodwind quintet
- a silk-screening fiber artist
- a sculptor who, with the students' help, created a permanent work of art on the campus

The Essence of Sliding

- a ceramicist
- a classical pianist and dramatist
- a photographer
- a musical duo, specializing in blues and ragtime.

The artists also helped the students in writing across the curriculum. For example, the last group of artists, the ragtime musical duo, helped fifth graders to write their own songs. In one class, the students wrote a poem called "Sometimes I Get So Mad"; in a different class, the students wrote "My Lonely Friend." The musicians then wrote the melody line for the songs and performed them later in the day for a school assembly.

Two middle school students, mentored by one of the poets, wrote the following poems, which were published in a school calendar of Native American poetry:

The Lonely Hogan

The lonely hogan sitting out
in the hot dry desert.
Far out in the distance
the lonely hogan is washed away
slowly with drops of rain,
tears running down her face,
washing the mud of the hogan away.
The lonely hogan still sitting
in the hot dry desert,
with a tear in her eye,
looking at the sunset over the mountain.
The lonely hogan still sitting
on the dry hot desert,
looking for some to live in her.

As I Walk

As I walk towards my grandma's house
In the corner of the beautiful canyon,
The fragrance of cottonwood twitches
My nose.

As I walk, I go into a dream.
I see my people, the Navajos,
Laboring in the cornfields,
Hot and sweaty.
An aroma of fried mutton
Passes my nose.

There are three ladies by a hogan
Cooking.
They are neatly dressed.
And their jewelry shines brightly
In the sun.

As I walk, I see a little Navajo girl.
She has soft brown eyes,
But they are filled with tears.
I pick her up
And put her on my knees.
She gives me a smile.

Field Trips

The primary objective of field trips was to take the students to the world. The trips, offering diverse educational experiences, were both mini- and maxi-excursions. Taking our students to the world enhanced their immersion in a rich language environment—an environment both at and away from the school.

We took short field trips to places and special events in the surrounding area (e.g., the Navajo Nation headquarters, the tribal zoo, the annual tribal fair, and the Navajo Tribal Chairman's inauguration). Longer trips involved going to places such as Denver, Dallas, Phoenix, San Diego, Los Angeles, and Carlsbad Caverns. A trip to Washington, DC, was designed especially for seven of our middle school student leaders, who participated for 1 week in a workshop for junior high school students from all over the country. Along with visiting all of the usual tourist attractions, the students saw the federal government at work by attending congressional sessions, committee meetings, and a Supreme Court session.

During the workshop, students participated in debates on governmental issues. Our students had never debated; in fact, they had never observed a debate. On the evening of the debate, however, five of our seven students participated. Our school had the highest percentage of debaters of all the schools, and our students were the only second language learners in the workshop.

Financing activities such as field trips and artists-in-residence is never easy. Wingate, like many other schools, faced budget cuts and tight money. However, the school administration established priorities for spending. By convincing the administration to scrimp in several areas, we were able to fund the programs we felt were essential to our curriculum goals. For example, we cut back on basal texts, ordering only what was absolutely necessary and purchasing no workbooks or commercially prepared dittoes.

Conclusion

We believe that the types of activities described above allowed the "essence of sliding" to emerge. Teachers did not attempt to *teach* "the essence of" anything. It evolved, instead, out of the rich language environment created by a variety of meaningful language activities.

"The essence of sliding" is what all of us are attempting to accomplish with our students, regardless of our area or level of work. We are striving to give our ESL learners the skills and knowledge they need to be proficient language users. If we design and facilitate their learning environments by using a whole language approach, ESL learners can become powerful, creative writers, like the eighth grader who wrote this poem:

> The Awaking
>
> Grandma gets up.
> She lights the stove
> that will fill my body
> with warmth.
> As she turns the doorknob
> with her aging hands,
> she looks at me
> and thinks of her youth.
> How good she felt
> in those days!
> Then in her soft voice
> she says,
> "Come here, grandson."
> Then slowly I walk towards her.
> We look at the sun slowly rising
> above the horizon
> of the great Navajo land.
> The she turns toward me
> and whispers, "Good-bye."
> As she says that
> her soft, warm lips
> gently kiss my forehead.
> Then she slowly walks towards
> the land that touches the sky.
> I know she will never come back.

4

Watson and Son's EFL Class

Teaching English to Chinese Children Using Only English and a U.S. Peer

Tim Watson

Tim Watson describes a beginning class of elementary school children aged 9–10 in Taiwan, Republic of China. What makes Watson's approach unusual is that he relies on his 11-year-old son as an assistant and peer tutor. He quickly discovers that both his Chinese ESOL students and his son benefit from the peer tutoring relationship.

Watson has been teaching English to kindergarten, elementary, junior high, and senior high school students in Taiwan since 1989.

I have discovered an effective and efficient way to teach English to Chinese elementary students without using any Chinese translation. I use my American son to model what I expect the students to do. This chapter is not a scientific study that compares and tests the effectiveness of peer modeling but a report on a teaching method I stumbled onto that has wonderful implications for the English as a foreign language (EFL) classroom. I will explain the theory and rationale for this class, discuss the benefits of peer modeling that I have observed, and show how I use a peer model in the classroom.

Watson and Son's EFL Class

Class Composition and Design

My class in Taiwan, Republic of China, consists of 14 elementary-aged students, 5 boys and 9 girls. Many of the students started the class as true beginners. They all attend Taiwan's public schools in Grades 2–6. My class, which meets twice a week in the evenings for 1 hour, is a private one that I organized at the request of the parents to help the children get ahead in English.

Private classes in most subjects abound in Taiwan because academic competition is so stiff. Entrance exams for college, high school, and even private junior high schools eliminate all but the best students. I also began teaching a class for the younger brothers and sisters of my students that meets an hour before the elementary-aged class. The parents want the little ones to get a head start, too.

Second language researchers have been telling teachers for several years that beginners need a silent time when they should not speak but only listen and follow instructions (Dulay, Burt, & Krashen, 1982; Postovsky, 1974). My son is a case in point. He attended Taiwan's public schools half a day for 18 months before he began speaking in Chinese. During those months of silence, he nodded, grunted, and responded using only one or two Chinese words. I alternated between losing confidence in the silent-period research and questioning my son's intelligence when suddenly, almost magically, he began to converse with friends using complete sentences.

Parents, the ones who pay for their children to be in my class, are not too fond of this idea of silence. They want their children to speak English right away. Parents feel that they are not getting their money's worth if their children can't say their name and age after the first month of classes, so I have compromised slightly and taught my students to answer a few simple questions and sing some songs. I have borrowed many ideas from the Total Physical Response approach (Asher, 1977) because it so effectively allows students to learn while remaining silent, but I also include songs and games in my instruction. Games and enjoyable activities create a happy, bouncy atmosphere in the classroom that keeps the children eager to come to class while creating an environment suitable for learning.

I have also designed the class with the belief that children will learn more naturally when the learners' native language is not used in the classroom. This is where my son comes in. By watching my son and me interacting, and by watching my son follow my instructions, my students are exposed to a more natural language environment.

Advantages of Peer Modeling

My 11-year-old son attends Chinese public school with some of the students in my class and knows all the others. I initially brought him to the class for two reasons. First, I look for as many ways as possible for us to spend time together, and having him help me teach my private classes gave me more time with him. Second, I thought he could take over instructing students. My voice often gives out while teaching high school students throughout the day, and during the evening classes I need my son to give the commands or ask questions.

Although I felt I needed him for my benefit, I quickly discovered that the students also benefited. They knew exactly what I wanted them to do when I told my son to do it first. They simply watched him and copied either his actions or his words. A fellow teacher who teaches a similar class once told me that her eager young students imitated everything she said. If she asked them to touch the red pen, they would look at her with big, innocent, confused eyes and say, "Touch the red pen." Then they would smile sheepishly without understanding that *they* should touch the red pen.

I found that I also confused the students if I tried to act out or explain what I wanted them to do. Few conversations involve only one person asking questions or giving commands and then responding. No wonder the children didn't understand; it's just not natural. I found, however, that if they watched me interact with my son, they had no problem understanding what they should do or say. I have continued to use modeling as a teaching tool to ensure that the students comprehend what they are to do, especially when I introduce something new or review something they have forgotten.

I later discovered more reasons to use my son in the classroom. Having my son there allows my students to hear another native speaker; most of the children have indicated that they prefer listening to *both* my son and me. Children imitate peers instead of adults or teachers when they are immersed in a new language (Burk, Lambert, & Tucker, 1975; Plann, 1977). My students study English only 2 hours a week—not quite an immersion program, but I think that the students feel more comfortable imitating a peer than they do an adult.

My son also occasionally assumes the role of teacher. After watching me teach a few times, he felt confident enough to allow me to split the class in half, with him taking one group and I, the other. Both groups usually worked on the same thing, but sometimes he engaged the students in a different activity. Either way, the students got more individual attention. His role in the class thus exceeds that of a model; he is really my assistant.

He also helps by contributing ideas for games and activities, some of which have been very successful, and by telling me when he thinks my ideas won't work. Because he has interests similar to those of the students, he has a good idea what they will enjoy or dislike—and he is usually right.

The peer assistant benefits from the experience, too. My son has claimed, "The main benefit is seeing the kids and talking to them." He usually plays with the students before and after class, which gives him more exposure to Chinese culture and language. He has also said, "I like going with *you*, Dad." I feel that the parent-child time we get during these two evenings a week helps bond us even closer. "I'm also learning how to teach," he stated proudly. He may never become a teacher, but teaching is a good skill to know. He has said that he is also learning to deal with students. "Most of the kids like me too," he continued, "so that makes it more fun." My son has begun to see the world from the perspective of a teacher, not just that of a student.

My 8-year-old son has also benefited from helping me teach. He recently began assisting me in a new class of 5- and 6-year-old children. I observed, and he reported on, some affective benefits that startled me. This son stutters, repeating one-syllable words, especially when he relates an experience, but he has not stuttered once while assisting me in class. He is a shy, quiet child, very different from his aggressive, outgoing older brother. Although he has been helping me only for a couple of months, he may have already profited more than his older brother has. In an interview, he said, "I like being with Dad and experiencing new things and being the boss. The kids want to learn and I like that. I like going for the money [he makes $1 per hour], but I like that the least. The kids try hard and are with us. They treat me as a teacher. I try my hardest to make them feel good. They respect me. I've always wanted that to happen. They do what I ask. It's fun to be important!" The good job my 8-year-old son has been doing in the class has boosted his sense of self-worth.

Peer Model's Roles

My son took on many roles initially and grew into others as his experience and confidence developed. In the beginning, he served as my helper by getting things for me, turning on the tape player or rewinding tapes, keeping score during contests, passing out names or colored papers, and handing me the puppet. All these simple chores eliminated time gaps during the lesson and kept the class moving. Although I could have done all these things myself, I felt his help and the time it saved justified his going to every class.

My son's most important role in this class now is modeling. In the beginning, he demonstrated uncomplicated things that any teacher could demonstrate (e.g., jumping or touching his nose). Later, he showed the students difficult responses that I could not figure out how to explain. For example, if I threw a pile of colored paper squares on the floor and asked for a blue paper or three greens and two reds, the students knew exactly what to do because they watched my son pick up the papers first. Although the students knew to touch their ears when I asked them to, they had no idea what I wanted them to do when the puppet asked, "Can I eat your ears?" But when my peer model demonstrated that a nod or a "yes" response got his ears chewed on by a puppet, and that a shake of the head or a "no" kept the puppet at bay, they became ecstatic because they now had the power to control whether or not the puppet chewed on them.

My peer model illustrated how to play a few games that would have been very difficult or impossible to explain without using Chinese. A modification of dodge ball, my assistant's idea, provided a great review of body parts. Two small teams faced each other holding different colored balls. My son or I called out the color of a ball to be thrown. If hit, the student had to say, "You hit my elbow," or whatever body part was hit. I hit the peer model a few times first so that all the students knew what they should say when they were hit.

My son gave me an idea for another game, Hide-and-Look, which taught all the objects in our classroom and reinforced some prepositions. When I asked, "Where is [my son's name] hiding?" they would respond by saying "under the phone" or "in the trash" (he actually stood with the phone on his head and stood in the trash can). My peer model also helped other students hide while the rest of us closed our eyes and counted to 10. Then we all looked for the hidden child from our seats. We could have done this activity by hiding an object, but letting the children hide themselves made everyone much happier.

Besides being a helper and a model, my son also assumed the role of small-group leader. The first few times we divided the class in half, he knew how to lead a group because he had just seen me do the same thing with the whole class. For example, he felt very comfortable asking students to put the big square in the yellow cup or to put their right hand under their left foot. One day, two new students who were about a year behind the others joined our class. I had so much confidence in my son's ability that I put him off with the two new students to help them learn colors, numbers, body parts, and a few prepositions. He knew how to teach these items because we had taught them together earlier. I gave him only minimal instructions, but I did keep an eye on him.

Later he took half the class and introduced brand-new activities. He bravely supervised a table full of peers who had to follow his instructions to make peanut-butter-and-jelly sandwiches. However, we stood back-to-back during this ordeal so that I could peek over my shoulder occasionally. When the students got too playful, he kept calm. Even the fact that I had to hurriedly move the laughing children back to their seats and change activities when things got really raucous didn't frustrate my assistant. He joined in laughing with them.

I also placed my peer assistant in the role of whole class leader. The students quickly recognized him as "Little Teacher," because from the first class meeting he would often take over the class. He seemed to enjoy calling one child to the front and telling her to touch the red car or to put three green pencils by the book. I suppose the class would have survived without his functioning as the class leader, but I think the students appreciated the variety.

After the students in the elementary-aged class were able to ask one another questions, my son became invaluable as a monitor. I often put the children in pairs to increase the amount of student talk. For example, once they could tell time in English, they asked each other when they ate breakfast, showered, or went to bed. My son always helped me monitor the pairs to make certain the students stayed on task and to see if they needed help. He often joined in the conversations because the things they discussed interested him. The students didn't just parrot memorized sentences; they told each other things that they had never said before in English. Nine-, 10-, and 11-year-old Chinese children who could speak no English just a few months before were communicating new information in English to their partners.

Because of my son's assistance, the students watched native English interaction and understood almost immediately what was expected of them. We freed the students from the frustration that comes with not understanding instructions, kept the class moving, and never needed to resort to translation into Chinese.

Applications

Other teachers should be able to apply the principles that I have found so rewarding. Those who teach in non-English-speaking countries may have difficulty locating a suitable peer assistant, but if they offer a small salary, native English-speaking expatriate children should be willing to help.

My eldest son moans when I have to take his younger brother to class for some reason because then he does not get his $1 per hour for helping me teach. I have often heard teachers say that if you want good teachers, you have to pay for them. The same is true of a good peer assistant. Teachers in English-speaking countries have a larger population of potential assistants, so they may be able to devise a less expensive reward system.

Training or preparation for peer assistants need not be too extensive. They should receive instruction on speaking clearly and more slowly at a level the whole class can hear. They also should know ahead of time to use as few words as possible and to keep them simple. They may need exact directions for responding to student questions so that they do not overwhelm students with unnecessary vocabulary. If they know beforehand the activities that will be taught, they should just respond naturally to the teacher's command or question.

If peer assistants know the first language of the students, as my son does, then they may need to know when it is appropriate to use the first language in the classroom. I have explained to my son that it is important to let the students learn naturally by observing and listening to us instead of relying on a Chinese explanation. I've told him that almost all students in Taiwan learn English through Chinese translation and that our method is special. So, even though he is often tempted to use Chinese, he does not because he understands the reasons for using English in the classroom.

The only other theory my son received before helping was, "Don't make 'em talk. Just let 'em point." He also knew ahead of time that he should assist me in every way he could.

Two important questions to ask about possible peer assistants are, "Will they do what I ask?" and "Can they control themselves?" I often emphasize the importance of my son's position so that he takes his job seriously and does not play idly in class. In almost every class there is some time during which he just sits and watches me teach. He occasionally gets distracted and jokes with the students in English during these times. A quick reminder of who he is or what his job is always supplies him with the needed "oomph" to act like an assistant instead of a rowdy student.

Conclusion

I have no hard evidence to prove that using a peer assistant to help teach and model my instructions has made my students learn faster, but it certainly makes my job much easier. Every one of my students has indicated that they felt it helped them to have my son in the class. They also claimed that they felt comfortable with my son assisting me. Within 9 months all the students could read primer materials and ask each other questions about what they had just read. This result, however, did not excite me as much as seeing the learners unafraid to use English, even to express new ideas. They also loved coming to class. I hope that they will *always* love studying English and maintain the attitude that English is enjoyable.

References

Asher, J. (1977). *Learning another language through actions: The complete teacher's guidebook.* Los Gatos, CA: Sky Oaks Productions.

Burk, M., Lambert, W., & Tucker, G. R. (1975). *Assessing functional bilingualism within a bilingual program: The St. Lambert project at grade eight.* Paper presented at the Ninth Annual TESOL Convention, Los Angeles.

Dulay, H., Burt, M., & Krashen, S. (1982). *Language two.* New York: Oxford University Press.

Plann, S. (1977). Acquiring a second language in an immersion classroom. In H. D. Brown, C. A. Yorio, & R. Crymes (Eds.), *Teaching and learning English as a second language: Trends in research and practice.* Washington, DC: Teachers of English to Speakers of Other Languages.

Postovsky, V. (1974). Effects of delay in oral practice at the beginning of second language learning. *Modern Language Journal, 58,* 5-6.

5

Teaching English in Russia

Alevtina Poliak

Among the profound changes that have recently taken place in the former Soviet Union is a heightening of interest in the learning and teaching of foreign languages, English in particular. In this chapter Alevtina Poliak suggests that knowledge of a foreign language (and access to a wider body of knowledge) altered people's thinking in the Soviet Union and prepared the way for glasnost *and* perestroika.

Poliak discusses the origins of her pedagogy and describes her experiences teaching English to young children. Her classroom in Russia contained jungle gym equipment, a large assortment of toys, and pictures of fruits, vegetables, clothing and flowers, which she used to enhance her lessons. She relied heavily on games and used the children's native language to help them develop conscious knowledge of how Russian works, knowledge that they could then transfer to their learning of English.

Poliak, who taught English to young children in Russia from 1962 to 1990, now lives in Corona, New York, USA.

In Russian schools, all children start learning a foreign language when they are 10 years old, generally attending two classes a week. Currently, English is the most popular foreign language.

Why the Increased Interest in Foreign Languages?

For decades, people in the Soviet Union lived in a state of informational isolation. Only books, newspapers, movies, and plays approved by Soviet officials were available. During the Stalinist period (1924–1953), any interest in Western literature or life would most likely place a person in conflict with the authorities and could result in being sentenced to a labor camp or to death. During the 1970s and 1980s Leonid Brezhnev's government, unlike that in the Stalinist period, neither encouraged nor punished an interest in Western culture.

At that time it was virtually impossible to find any pertinent information in Russian on any subject outside the accepted and official culture (e.g., non-Marxist philosophy, history, yoga, astrology, or modern Western culture). People who knew a foreign language were lucky as they could listen to foreign broadcasting and read foreign publications.

Educated Soviet people began using any means possible to obtain information about the world outside the Soviet Union. Many people voluntarily translated articles and passed them around among their friends and colleagues. People with any information outside the official ideology enjoyed particular respect. Knowledge of a foreign language opened a window onto a different world. I believe that this informal flow of information gradually changed the consciousness of Soviet society, which ceased viewing itself as an isolated entity and began to see itself as part of the international community.

With the advent of *perestroika* (1986–1991), the Soviet people had an opportunity to go abroad and read foreign magazines and newspapers. At the same time, more foreigners began to visit the Soviet Union. Knowledge of a foreign language became more of a necessity rather than something of a luxury. Despite these developments, I do not attribute the increased interest in foreign languages to *perestroika*. It is not *perestroika* that has affected interest in foreign languages; instead, an increased interest in teaching and learning foreign languages has helped to change people's thinking, thereby preparing the ground for *glasnost* and *perestroika*.

The increased interest in foreign languages that preceded *perestroika* was apparent at the end of the 1970s. In Moscow, Leningrad, and other big cities, language classes for both adults and children emerged, sponsored by various federal and private clubs and associations. Parents wanted their children to study foreign languages in order to have opportunities they had missed while growing up.

Foreign language teaching in the Soviet Union at that time was devoid of any ties to experiential or historical realities. Students learned grammar and vocabulary that was unconnected to real-life experiences. Around the Soviet Union, both children and adults learned English with the help of almost identical texts, which all began with the sentences *This is a table* and *This is a map*. As foreign language learning became more popular, so-called intensive methods of foreign language teaching became fashionable. *Suggestopedia*, the first intensive learning methodology, developed by Georgi Lozanov, was brought from Bulgaria. In classes where teachers used Lozanov's method, learning was very lively: Students listened to popular music, role played, and looked at films and slides, and teachers offered a great deal of information about foreign countries. Lozanov's methodology became very popular among both teachers and students. Teachers from all over the country began to discuss which methods were more effective: the new or the old.

Negnevitskaya's Method

It is within this context that my colleague, Elena Negnevitskaya, created an interesting and effective language teaching methodology for children. Negnevitskaya graduated from Moscow University in 1970 and began to work at the children's club *Orlenok* (Little Eagle), which was attached to Moscow University. Negnevitskaya's association with the university allowed her to avoid working in the federal education system, which was tightly controlled and regulated. Consequently, she did not have to implement obligatory programs but worked independently and experimented with her own methodology throughout the 1970s. The use of games as an educational tool is at the center of her methodology.

Negnevitskaya believes that the best age to begin studying a language is 5 years, but she accepts students as young as 3 and as old as 9. Negnevitskaya's method consists of three stages. In the first stage, which lasts for about a year, only oral language is used. The second stage lasts for about half a year, during which the students express themselves in writing. Instead of using regular spelling, however, they write phonetic transcriptions of words. Negnevitskaya believes that this stage is important in the acquisition of a foreign language because it leads to an understanding of the phonetic structure and sound system of the foreign language. During the third stage students both read and write. The children's knowledge of basic spoken language and its phonetic transcription makes it easier to learn how to read and spell.

After the first year of study, the children can discuss a number of familiar topics (e.g., modes of transportation, food, clothing, furniture, animals, shopping) using basic English. The children learn the colors and can count to 100. In the area of grammar, they learn the singular and plural forms of nouns, can form a question, and know the simple present and present continuous tenses. After 2 years of study, the children can read simple texts, and their vocabulary increases to the level at which they can stage little plays. In the area of grammar, they master the present perfect tense.

Use of the Native Language

Negnevitskaya's method differs somewhat from other methods used today. Although many teachers try to exclude the native language while teaching a foreign language, Negnevitskaya does not believe in this practice. Because her students do not live in an English-speaking environment and have only two short English classes each week, she believes that using the native language can speed up learning.

Speak the Native Language With a "Foreign" Accent

At the beginning of their studies, children do not know many English words, but they must acquire English pronunciation as soon as they begin to learn the language. The children therefore play a game in which they pretend they are foreigners who don't know Russian very well; they try to pronounce the Russian words and sentences with an English accent. This exercise amuses the children and creates an awareness of the sound differences between languages.

Grammatical Analysis of the Target Language

Before embarking on the study of English grammar, the children perform grammatical analyses of their native tongue, Russian, which Negnevitskaya feels they have usually mastered by the age of 5. However, children's knowledge of the grammar of their native language is hidden in their subconscious minds. For example, when asked how to form the plural of nouns or what tenses exist in their native language, children are unlikely to be able to explain. Moreover, they will probably not even understand the question. If one states the question properly, however, children are capable of giving an answer.

For example, I asked children to tell me when I was naming many objects in Russian and when I named only one. Naturally, the children guessed correctly. I pretended to be surprised and asked them how they knew, as I had not shown them the objects but had only named them. Although the children were often surprised at their knowledge and had difficulty explaining how they knew, someone usually found the answer:

The words in plural have another sound at the end. "Yes," I would say, "in Russian the sound [i] is the sign that the word means *many*." Then I told them that the English language has other signs indicating plurality (the [s] and [z] sounds).

Games: The Method in Action

The main idea underlying Negnevitskaya's methodology is that children, in contrast with adults, are not motivated to learn a foreign language unless placed in a foreign environment. Therefore, the teacher's main goal is to create the motivation, usually by constructing lessons that consist of a series of games. Children like to play and are eager to win. The teacher arranges the games in such a way that the children learn the language in the process of playing. Any one game lasts for only a short time, as young children cannot concentrate on a single issue for a long time. Because little children cannot sit still for long, it is important to use games that involve movement. The games are designed to pursue different goals, such as learning vocabulary, practicing grammar, or perfecting pronunciation.

Circus

In the Circus game, played in the very first lesson, the goal is to understand such commands as *jump, run, climb,* and *stand up*. The children pretend to be trained animals from Australia; therefore, they can understand only English commands. The teacher is a trainer, and the room is a circus. The trainer gives one command to all of the "animals," and those who perform the command correctly receive an award. When the children do not understand the command, the trainer demonstrates the action. Very soon all the children are performing the commands correctly. Then the teacher gives a command to each "animal" individually. When the children understand the commands well, each of them in turn becomes the trainer.

The game becomes more and more complicated as the children master it. The teacher shows them some toy animals and names them: for example, *a rabbit, a bear, a duck, a monkey*. Each child is assigned the role of a specific animal. Then the teacher gives a command to a specific animal (e.g., "The Fox must jump!" or "The Bear, please stand up!"). The children respond by acting out the animal they represent.

Hidden Toy

When the children are studying a group of nouns such as clothes, furniture, animals, or vehicles, they play the Hidden Toy game. The children are divided into two teams. All the toys are placed on the table. The teacher says, "Look and remember." Then the children leave the room, and the teacher hides one of the toys. In a few minutes the children return to the room. The child who guesses which toy is missing brings victory to his or her team.

Shopping

This game is suitable for the entire course of study. The word units involved in the game grow in complexity throughout the course:

>Give me a ...
>Give me a red bear.
>Give me the big red bear.
>Give me those two green birds and a small white rabbit.

At first the teacher plays the part of the salesperson and the children are the customers. Toys are the merchandise. The children already know the names of the toys, but the game helps them to learn expressions such as, *Give me ...*, *Can I help you?*, *You're welcome*, and *Thank you*. By the end of the school year, the children are capable of conducting a rather well-developed dialogue.

Guess What I Am

When the students know a fair number of words, they begin making riddles. To start the game, the teacher pretends to be an animal and describes it using familiar vocabulary: "I am big. I am brown. I eat honey." "It's a bear!" exclaims a student. The teacher says, "OK, it's a bear. Now the winner makes up another riddle." The child says, "I am grey. I am small. I have a tail." If nobody knows the answer, the child continues, "I can run. I can jump. I eat cheese and bread." If nobody knows the answer yet, the class asks the child questions: "Can you swim?" "Can you fly?" "Can you climb?" "You are an elephant," exclaims one of the children. "Why?" "You are grey." "No," says the winner triumphantly, "I am a mouse."

The Role of Parents

The majority of children come to classes accompanied by adults. Unlike most teachers, Negnevitskaya likes parents to be present during the classes. Following her example, I found the parents' presence to be very helpful to the children's learning. First, the parents learned what the children were studying and could later review the material with their children at home. Second, the parents' presence during the competitive games stimulated and inspired the participants.

Conclusion

Elena Negnevitskaya was the first educator in Russia to apply knowledge of psycholinguistics and psychology to the teaching of a foreign language. She developed a method of teaching based on two ideas: that speech is part of the communication process and that games play an important educational role for children. As a result, Negnevitskaya's method is full of life and excitement and highly effective.

6

Teaching English in Primary Schools in Brunei Darussalam

Ng Seok Moi and Wendy Preston

Brunei Darussalam, a small, independent sultanate with a population of about 270,000, lies on the northeast coast of Borneo. Although Brunei Darussalam is a Malay-speaking country, English assumes an important place in the education of its students. For the first 3 years of primary school, Malay is the language of instruction and English is a school subject. Afterward, English becomes the medium of instruction for most school subjects.

In 1989 the Brunei Ministry of Education, impressed by the success of a Singapore English language program, invited Ng Seok Moi to develop a similar program, now known as RELA (Reading and Language Acquisition), as a new way of teaching English in the first 3 years of primary school. Wendy Preston joined the project in 1991. In this chapter they outline the philosophy and approach of the RELA project and describe a typical week of ESL instruction in a Brunei classroom full of children actively involved in learning English the RELA way.

Brunei Darussalam is warm and humid, so windows in the classroom are usually wide open. Overhead fans create a welcome movement of the air, which by midday has become undeniably hot. A feature of the capital city of Brunei Darussalam is its "water village"—almost a city within a city—built on stilts over the waters of the wide Brunei river. In some schools, there is water, not grass, outside the classroom. One can hear the swish of water taxis outside, and a plop rather than a thud if anything is sent through a window.

The children in the lower primary classes are bubbly, active 6- to

―――――――― Common Threads of Practice ――――――――

10-year-olds. The average number of pupils per class is 25, although occasionally there may be only 5 or 6 children in a class in rural areas. Pupils wear school uniforms. For the boys the uniform is white shirts and dark shorts; they sometimes wear the round Malay *songkok*, a piece of adult headgear that somehow makes them look both grown up and mischievous. The girls wear white blouses and dark tunics for the first year or two, though soon they will be grown up enough to wear the ankle-length, pastel-checked skirt and long-sleeved, knee-length white top that is the schoolgirl version of the *baju kurung*—the elegant dress worn by Malay women. With it, they will wear the *tudung*, a carefully folded white scarf that hides every strand of hair.

Because Brunei Darussalam is a Muslim state, where the religious influence is strong, boys and girls are usually grouped separately for most of their lessons, with the boys sitting in rows at the front of the class and the girls behind. The Reading and Language Acquisition (RELA) programme has, however, been able to modify the traditional classroom seating arrangement somewhat to provide for group learning that is more conducive to language acquisition. Although our learning environment tends to be more relaxed than that in other classes, with children moving around according to the activities in which they are engaged, boys and girls still tend to want to be grouped separately.

Our classroom arrangement provides an open space for shared reading and for language experience activities, as well as places for paper-and-pencil tasks. The RELA classroom normally has an area at one end of the room where all the children can gather and sit on the floor for reading and oral work. Writing and drawing activities deriving from that work are conducted in group "corners," at tables with chairs around them.

The schedule provides for an hour of English each day. We include a variety of activities in each lesson to ensure that there will be movement from the story area at the front, to the group-work stations, and to other locations in the classroom for activities such as individual reading or language games.

Program Design and Philosophy

The following concepts have guided the development of the RELA program:

1. Language is best acquired in a meaningful setting.
2. Children learn efficiently when they are interested.

3. Interest in reading is fostered through access to an abundant supply of appropriate, well-illustrated, well-written storybooks.

4. Language skills, both receptive and expressive, are best learnt in an integrated manner.

RELA uses several teaching methods to make these concepts come to life in the classroom. Chief among these is the Shared Book approach, which is reinforced with supplementary language activities.

The idea behind the Shared Book approach (Holdaway, 1979) is similar to that of story reading at bedtime, but transplanted to the classroom. The approach highlights the meaning and enjoyment that books provide. Because most children love to hear stories, love being read to and, in due course, take pride in the ability to read books themselves, the Shared Book approach is our starting point for teaching English.

Most children enjoy reading and rereading a story. The repetition is a way of letting them absorb the language and its meaning. In first language acquisition, unforced, naturally occurring repetition is an indispensable element, and the Shared Book approach is based on what we know about the home background of children who learn to read easily. Such children have already had books before they come to school. Their parents have read to them, and they have seen people at home reading newspapers and books. We see the Shared Book approach as one way of providing shared reading opportunities for children who may not have had much acquaintance with books in their homes. The repeated reading of a story from a picture book, we think, is one of the most likely ways of allowing the phrases in the book to become established in the memory and to be assimilated.

Big 46- by 61-cm (18- by 24-inch), attractive storybooks with colourful pictures and clearly printed text are used to introduce new stories to the children. We prop these Big Books on an easel to allow a whole class of children to see the pictures and text. The children are always invited to join in the rereadings of the stories and, through these repetitions, learn language in a nonthreatening and enjoyable atmosphere.

The books are specially selected for their story lines, visual appeal, and language development potential as well as their cultural appropriateness. All of the books selected for use in the programme must conform to the country's religious doctrines and practices. Because few local stories are written in English, most of the stories are imports from outside the local experience. They include both traditional Anglo-European favourites like *The Three Billy Goats Gruff* (1987) and more recent publications such as Joy Cowley's *I'm the King of the Mountain* (Cowley, 1984). Plans are under way to produce books that will use local stories to lend a more distinctively Bruneian flavour to the children's reading experiences.

Because we are teaching English as a second, spoken language, we have incorporated another element into our lessons: the language experience element. Here the children meet again some of the vocabulary and structures first seen in the storybooks and practice them in a different context. Language experience activities begin with one that pupils watch, listen to, take part in, discuss, draw pictures of, and, finally, write about.

A Week in the RELA Programme

What is it like to be a teacher or student in the RELA programme? We operate on 5-day cycles that permit us to introduce, practice, reinforce, and review material over a period of time. Below we describe a typical week in a year 2 class, with children aged 7–8 years.

It is the first day of the cycle, and the children are pouring into the classroom. They stand as we exchange greetings, then arrange themselves on the mat at the front of the classroom.

We have a new book, which we shall be reading for the first time today. But first we sing a song and read an old favourite book: *I'm the King of the Mountain* (Cowley, 1984), *Sleepy on Sunday* (Graham & Gynell, 1988), or *In the Middle of the Night* (Graham, 1988).

Halimah is sitting quietly attentive, so I invite her to choose. She selects *I'm the King of the Mountain*, and I place it on the easel. Most of the children know this story by heart, but 25 pairs of eyes still eagerly scan the pictures and the text and laugh over the funny bits. Seeing the drawings again and rereading the text reinforces the relationship between the writing, the meaning, and the sound of the words. Even Ali and Fatimah, who have had some difficulty with English, are joining enthusiastically in the refrain:

> "I'm the King of the Mountain."
> "I'm the King of the Mountain."

Ali, I note with satisfaction, is now able to read the full refrain.

It is time for the new book, a moment of excitement and anticipation. I bring it out, and all eyes focus on the tantalising picture on the cover—

a bright green jungle panorama of waving fronds and huge leaves, with a row of monkeys sitting on a branch. One of the monkeys is reaching up for a big blue butterfly fluttering past; another turns his face toward us, as if to invite us to join the animals in their leafy jungle world. We discuss the cover: Who has seen a monkey? What are these monkeys doing? Where are they? What do they do all day? What will the story be about? As we look at the cover and talk about it, the children try to imagine what the content of the story will be.

We have a lot to talk about in each book—things we know already, things we don't know. During the first reading the children sit quietly, listen, and watch while I use my pointer to pick out the words as I read. At the end of the first page there are usually more questions to think and talk about: What does the book say the monkeys are doing? What happened to them? What will happen next? Let's see whose guess is right! Already a few of the children are joining in as they catch sight of recognisable words.

We read the story through again. This time, as I point to the words and read, more of the children join in, remembering what they have just heard, using the pictures for reference, and identifying words they already know. I try to watch the children as we read together. First, I watch their reactions to the story. Then I watch to see whether most of the children are joining in with the shared reading or whether some of them need more help.

With the children still sitting on the floor in the front of the classroom, we begin to extend our use of some of the language we have seen in the story. The children relate what we have read to their own lives. We concentrate on certain language items, try to reactivate vocabulary learnt earlier, and bring newly met words into active use.

Today we finish with a worksheet connected with the story. There is a hum of activity as the children write or colour. I walk round checking work and giving individual attention where it is needed.

On the 2nd day of the cycle we begin by rereading the story that was introduced on Day 1. It contains some new words and some important old ones that I want the children to focus on. We have an adjustable mask—a cardboard window with a panel that can be moved to make the slot longer or shorter. I use the mask to highlight some of these words, one by one. "What is this word?" Lots of hands are up.

"Ali, tell us."
"Cookie."
"Yes, that's right! Now can you find a word that rhymes with *keep*?"

Common Threads of Practice

Othman comes to the front and outlines *sheep* in the mask. Then we do it the other way round. "Who can show me the word *scissors*?" I ask. I choose a child to come to the front, find the word on the page, and highlight it with the mask. Gradually the stock of words the children recognise and understand is increasing.

On the first 2 days of the cycle, language input has come primarily from the Big Book stories. On Days 3 and 4 our lessons start in the same way as before, with the repetition of something familiar, whether a song, a poem, or some of the stories we read earlier. We also reread the week's Big Book. After the "tuning in" on Days 3 and 4, however, the lesson moves in a different direction. We do not discuss the story itself anymore but select structures from it to practise in their own right and in a different context. For instance, if we have seen words like *sugar, bananas,* and *sweets* mentioned in the Big Book, we may choose expressions of quantity as a language item to practise.

With a few props I create a simple market stall background on top of a table. With a large MARKET sign, some scales for measuring, and a few grocery items such as a kilogram of sugar, a packet of sweets, and a bunch of bananas, we're ready to start. Within this miniscenario, the class and I then develop a simple dialogue between a customer and a shopkeeper.

Customer:	Good morning, Awang Kadir.
Shopkeeper:	Good morning, Dayang Azizah.
Customer:	May I have a kilo of bananas, please?
Shopkeeper:	(weighing) Here is a kilo of bananas.
Customer:	May I have four apples, please?
Shopkeeper:	Here are four apples.
Customer:	Thank you. (pretends to pay and leave)

We repeat the dramatization, allowing several children to have a turn and changing the items bought and sold.

The language we are focusing on today has been introduced as spoken dialogue. Because our aim is to establish the link between speaking, reading, and writing, we strengthen the connection by recording the conversation in the market. The children are sitting on the mat at the front of the classroom. I tape a clean sheet of newsprint to the blackboard, and we recall what we have just been doing. "What shall we call our writing today?" "Shopping," someone suggests, so I write this as a heading in large print on the paper. "Azizah, you wanted to buy some bananas. Where did you go?" "I went to the market." As the children answer my questions, I write their responses on the paper:

> I went to the market. I bought a kilo of bananas. I also bought some apples.
> I paid the shopkeeper. Then I went home.

The class has, in effect, dictated a composition, and has watched the spoken words become writing. After I have written down the children's simple account of our activity, we read it aloud from the sheet of paper.

The children now go back to their work corners. Each group chooses two grocery items, and I ask them to write a group story, similar to the one that the class dictated, using the items. Working together, each group produces a story and usually an illustration. When a group finishes a story, the class reads aloud what they have written. There is pride in the voices of the children as they read the compositions they have created.

On Day 4 we take the process one step further: The children each write their own story based on the previous day's preparation. I have brought pictures of things that we can buy in the market. We look at the pictures, name the items, and talk about them. I write the words on the board. We have seen most of the words before, and this is a chance to review them. The children choose two items they would like to purchase and go off to write their stories.

Day 5 brings a change in the routine. Though we start the lesson in the usual way, with some shared reading and a song, the rest of the lesson period takes on a different configuration. On the first 4 days, the children work in mixed-ability groups on the premise that there will be important interaction between the children whose English is strong and those who are less advanced in the language. On Day 5, the children are divided into groups according to their ability and have a chance to go faster or more slowly on more specific tasks. Each group concentrates on a particular language task for 10 or 15 minutes; then the groups switch places or activities.

The activities consist of Book Corner, Word Bank, and Listening Post. Children go to the Book Corner, which contains a plentiful supply of normal-sized books, to read independently. Small versions of the Big Books that we have read in class are found there, as well as some other storybooks. I always have one or two new books to add to those already on the shelves. I show these new books to the children at the beginning of the lesson and talk a little about each one, hoping that someone will be tempted to dip into it. We call this generous supply of books, which is crucial to our RELA project, the Book Flood, after the experiment conducted in Fiji (Elley & Manghubai, 1983). We want to offer a torrent of good material to the children so that reading always presents itself as a pleasant prospect to them.

—————— **Common Threads of Practice** ——————

The Listening Post consists of a tape recorder and several sets of earphones. I have recorded all the Big Books we have read onto tapes and have taught the pupils how to find the right book, switch on the recorder, and read along with the voice on the tape. In this way, children can choose their favourite books and hear them as often as they like, following the words in the book as they hear the story. The Book Corner and Listening Post provide flexibility to the class, allowing children to work independently and at their own speed.

In the third activity, the Word Bank, the children make word cards that they keep in a box—the "banks." As the children collect word cards, they are also storing up the knowledge that the cards represent, so that eventually they will own the words themselves, words that they can identify and write. I begin by distributing copies of the class-dictated writing from Day 3. The children underline the words they know, then copy them into a notebook, whose pages we have arranged in alphabetical order. From the notebook, the words are copied onto 3- by 7-cm (1- by 2 3/4-inch) cards.

The notebook becomes the child's personal dictionary, and the cards are used to play a variety of word games: matching pictures to words, arranging the cards in alphabetical order, and sorting them into separate categories such as colour words or the names of animals. In such games the children are learning, without conscious effort, to identify the words at a glance. A variety of reading and writing activities reinforce learning.

Findings From the RELA Programme

Like any other programme or approach, RELA depends enormously on individual teachers for its success. The effectiveness of each lesson depends on the teacher's ability to present it with an immediacy and liveliness that will capture the children's imagination and willingness to participate.

When we first introduced RELA to local Bruneian teachers, we were apprehensive as to whether they would be willing to adapt to this new approach. Though more stimulating and more attuned to the age level and natural learning behaviour of primary school children than the traditional textbook method used previously in Brunei Darussalam, the RELA method was nevertheless quite a departure from the methods teachers had previously used. After 3 years of operation, however, the feedback from teachers has been encouraging. Teachers report that, although they have to work harder with the RELA approach, they prefer it to their former method of teaching English. Most would like to see RELA become the accepted method of teaching primary school English.

RELA techniques have been formally evaluated in two separate studies in Brunei Darussalam (Ng, 1992a; 1992b). Both showed RELA children outperforming their peers in the four language skills: listening, speaking, reading, and writing. RELA students are also visibly more at home with books than are children whose main contact with the printed word in English has been through a single textbook. These results are consistent with the opinions of teachers who have taught in the programme and of outside observers who have visited RELA classes.

Official support for the programme has been a welcome and necessary factor in the programme's success. Substantial funding was needed for books and other equipment, as well as for personnel to implement the programme in the classroom. A dedicated team of local project officers served as catalysts for change in these primary school classrooms in Brunei Darussalam, a change that has made English language learning a more worthwhile and enjoyable experience for many children.

References

Cowley, J. (1984). *I'm the king of the mountain*. Wellington, New Zealand: School Publications Branch, Department of Education.

Elley, W. B., & Manghubai, F. (1983). The impact of reading on second language learning. *Reading Research Quarterly, 19* (1).

Graham, A. (1988). *In the middle of the night*. Australia: Era Publications.

Graham, A., & Gynell, D. (1988). *Sleepy on Sunday*. Australia: Era Publications.

Holdaway, D. (1979). *The foundation of literacy*. Sydney: Ashton Scholastic.

Ng, Seok Moi. (1992a). *Improving English language learning for young speakers of other languages*. Unpublished paper presented at the IRA World Congress on Reading, Maui, HI.

Ng, Seok Moi. (1992b). *The thirteenth consultant report on the Reading and Language Acquisition Project*. Report presented to the Ministry of Education, Brunei Darussalam.

The three billy goats gruff. (1987). New York: Scholastic/TAB Publications.

Additional Readings

Ashton-Warner, S. (1983). *Teacher*. London: Secker & Warburg.

Lee, D. M., & Allen, R. V. A. (1963). *Learning to read through experience*. Englewood Cliffs, NJ: Prentice-Hall.

Ng, Seok Moi. (1988). *Research into children's language and reading development*. Singapore: Institute of Education.

7

Learning English Naturally in Emelie Parker's Classroom

Sue Sherman

Sue Sherman has taught art to children in Europe, Asia, Africa, and the United States. As a student in a teacher preparation program at George Mason University, Fairfax, Virginia, USA, she visited Emelie Parker's first-grade classroom on several occasions. In this chapter she describes what she saw during those visits.

Parker teaches at an elementary school in Falls Church, Virginia, where a majority of the students are nonnative speakers of English. Although a large number of Parker's students are ESOL learners, they manage quite well in the classroom. Sherman concludes that the reason for their success is the experiential nature of the learning activities that Parker uses in her classroom.

Emelie Parker teaches at Bailey's Elementary School in the city of Falls Church, Virginia. The school draws its students from a neighborhood that is culturally diverse: 80% of the students speak English as a second language (ESL), and Emelie's class reflects the ethnic mix of the school community. Although English is the second language for 19 of her 25 students, they are able to function and communicate in the classroom with great success and enthusiasm. The students speak Urdu, Cambodian, Somali, Vietnamese, and Spanish at home. One Vietnamese boy, Tam, had arrived from Vietnam 1 month before I visited the class. He had started at Bailey's Elementary School only 3 days before I met him and spoke no English.

― Common Threads of Practice ―

Emelie Parker's Approach to Learning

When I visited Emelie's classroom, I noticed that she used whole language teaching strategies that integrated speaking, reading, writing, thinking, and listening throughout the day. The classroom was a language-learning center where language was used across the curriculum (e.g., in math, science, music, social studies, art, and language arts) and in the many activities in which the children engaged. Emelie reinforced her ESL students' acquisition of English while they learned other subjects. After visiting the class, I concluded that whole language teaching techniques were particularly well suited to teaching ESL students in a regular classroom setting.

The Setting

At one end of Emelie's classroom is a Sharing Corner where students gather in small groups or as a class. Books are arranged on shelves so that their covers are easily seen. There are pillows and a few stuffed animals. On the wall is the Classroom Bill of Rights, which says, "I have the right to be happy, to be safe, to be heard, to learn about myself, to be myself." There is also a Student of the Week table, where students can browse through photographs, awards, a favorite toy, and the flag of the country of the student of the week (each student is honored in turn). Students can leave notes for Emelie in a tiny red mailbox. All these items serve to affirm the students' importance and increase their self-esteem while giving them opportunities to learn about and share in each others' cultures and experiences.

At the other end of the classroom are low tables where students have assigned seats. At each table are at least one native English speaker, one nonnative English speaker with strong reading and writing skills, and two ESL students. This arrangement allows the native English-speaking student and the strong reader-writer to benefit from being peer teachers and the ESL students to profit from working with strong readers and writers and native English speakers. On each table are containers of pencils, crayons, and markers. Near the tables are low shelves that hold a variety of materials, including math materials, boxes for student journals, and writing folders. All are set within easy reach of students. Above the shelves are large, low windows; plants thrive on the windowsill. Students' paintings and written work fill the walls. On a low table near the classroom door students put flowers and treasures brought in for Show and Tell.

As her students come into the room, Emelie greets each by name and comments on what they are wearing or carrying. One day two girls bring flowers and another brings candy from her country in Latin America. By speaking meaningfully and personally to each student, Emelie again affirms the worth of each individual, and models native English speaking. Students are learning and creating language through natural social interaction.

The students put away their coats and bags as they chat among themselves. Six of them go to the tables with their writing folders and, working in twos, give each other spelling tests. Each student chooses the spelling words for the tests according to his or her own writing needs. The rest of the class goes to the Sharing Corner, where they sit on the carpet talking with Emelie and each other. When the spellers have finished their tests, they bring them to Emelie, who congratulates them on their results and encourages all the children to sound out the incorrectly spelled words. By having her students work cooperatively on their spelling, Emelie is helping them to work more independently and responsibly.

When all the children have assembled on the carpet, they go through daily routines, saying the date and the type of weather expected for the day. The daily announcements heard over the school's loudspeaker speak to the multicultural nature of the school: "Bailey's Elementary School is a school for all nations; let us pledge allegiance to the flag of the country that brings us together through freedom." Through this simple daily message, Bailey's Elementary School recognizes and celebrates the rich cultural diversity of its students.

Science Lesson

After the announcements, the class gets ready for a science lesson on the fastest way to make compost. Emelie begins, "Today we will be doing a scientific experiment. Who can tell me what they know about scientific experiments?" By asking this question, she allows the children to make connections between what they already know and what they will be learning. She captures their interest and makes them feel confident about tackling new learning. As the students talk about scientists testing medicines and toothpastes before they are sold in stores, Emelie records their comments on the blackboard, visually reinforcing what the children are saying.

―――――― **Common Threads of Practice** ――――――

The discussion of scientific experiments leads to an explanation of the scientific method, which, Emelie explains, is a method used everywhere in the world. She points to a chart that she has made:

SCIENTIFIC METHOD
(1) STATE THE PROBLEM: we want to find out...
(2) WRITE THE HYPOTHESIS: we think...
(3) DESIGN THE EXPERIMENT: we will test...
(4) RECORD AND ANALYZE DATA
(5) DRAW CONCLUSIONS

The chart visually reinforces what the class is talking about and expresses new ideas in concise terms. A student writes a list of what the class wants to know more about on a large pad of paper (e.g., "What is the fastest way to make compost?").

Emelie asks Tam, the newly arrived student from Vietnam, to write the numbers 1, 2, 3, and 4 on four pieces of paper; these numbered papers will eventually label the four boxes of compost. Emelie asks the student beside Tam to help him. She then makes another chart indicating the four methods they will use to establish the fastest way to make compost: air and water added, air only added, water only added, and neither air nor water added. She then asks the students to predict which way will be the fastest. The children vote, and the results are recorded on the chart. Their recorded votes serve to reinforce their predictions. Emelie and the students place bags of dead leaves, grass cuttings, rotten cabbage leaves, carrots, and fertilizer on a big sheet. As Emelie holds up each item, the students call out its name; some children explain its use. They then take turns measuring and pouring the compost ingredients into each of the four boxes.

The students start to become restless at this point, so Emelie asks them to move to their tables in order to give them a change of setting. She carries the four boxes of compost materials to the tables and asks the students to predict whether the temperature in the boxes would vary if they were to stir the compost materials. Emelie tells them to rub their hands together and asks them how their hands feel. They notice that their hands have become warmer. She then suggests that the motion of rubbing their hands makes heat and asks them if they think the compost that was stirred would be warmer or cooler than that which was not. They decide that it would get warmer, just as their hands had. This exercise is a good example of building student comprehension through physical response.

Throughout the science lesson the students use all aspects of language as they listen, think, read, write, and speak at their own language levels. Not only are they learning about conducting a science experiment on composting, but they are also making meaning with language in a context-embedded learning experience. Their experience with concrete material reinforces the meaning of the words they are learning and using: they understand the words because they talk about what they are doing as they are doing it.

Math Lesson

The 7-year-old students, who have concentrated and worked hard for more than an hour, are noisy and restless after their science lesson. Emelie asks them to put their heads on their tables so that they can calm down and get ready for math. Once the class is calm, two students distribute math boards and boxes of wooden sticks and cubes, which represent units of 10s and 1s respectively. Emelie turns on the overhead projector and begins to write and talk: "Farmer Brown let 16 chickens into the road. How many 10s is that? Good! Put one *10s* stick on your board. How many ones? Good! Put six *1s* cubes on your board." She places one 10s stick and six 1s cubes on the overhead projector so that the students can see what she is talking about. They do the same on their boards. They continue working on the problem, talking it through. Throughout the discussion of the math problem, the students' senses are engaged as they listen to what Emelie and their classmates are saying, watch what Emelie is doing, manipulate the math cubes and sticks, and write the numbers.

Then Emelie says, "We're going to play teacher. When you are the teacher, what do you need to do?" Several hands shoot up. The students explain that the teachers have to make up stories for their math problems and talk through their problems with the rest of the class. Emelie chooses one student to be the first teacher and four others to be dice rollers (the numbers rolled on the dice determine which numbers will be used in the math problem). Emelie chooses new teachers and rollers after each math problem until all the students have had a turn.

A Vietnamese girl volunteers to be the teacher. She whispers her story to the class. Emelie sits down and hugs her, telling her that she has told a beautiful story that everyone would like to hear and asking her to tell it more loudly, which the girl does. These sentences are the first the girl has spoken in front of the class. Emelie asks the girl if she would like to go down the hall and tell her ESL teacher so they can celebrate what she has done.

———————— Common Threads of Practice ————————

Classroom Management

Ready to read aloud a story about air, Emelie says, "Get into your listening positions." Several students need to be reminded again, and she comments, "Tam (the newly arrived Vietnamese boy) will learn from seeing what you do. Right now he can't understand what I'm saying, but he will learn what I am saying by seeing how you sit to get ready for listening." Here Emelie turns a discipline lapse into a positive experience for the students, encouraging them to model behavior for Tam so that he can understand what he is expected to do.

Note-Taking Lesson

Emelie then reminds the students that they had been talking about air that morning in their science lesson. As she reads the story about air, she asks questions to check the students' comprehension. When she comes to the word *valley*, she makes the shape of a valley with her arms and asks them to do the same. Next Emelie tells her students that she is going to teach them how to take notes for the independent reports they are preparing on dinosaurs and other topics. To find out what the students already know about note taking, she asks them two questions: "What does it mean to take notes? Who takes notes?" Emelie then takes out a book about dandelions, explaining that it is a nonfiction book that she is going to read for information. Next she says, "Now I'm going to model what I want you to do. While I'm reading the book, I'm going to talk about what I'm thinking and you are going to try to find out what's going on in my brain. Your job is to listen." In this way Emelie states clearly what the students must do.

She begins reading the book aloud, modeling fluent reading and reading for a purpose (in this case, to get information). After reading each page, she asks herself, "What is important for me to know on this page?" Then she writes phrases on large paper so that all her students can see how to take notes:

NOTES:

Things I need to understand
  Things I don't know
  Ideas, thoughts, facts that are important to share (e.g., dandelion flowers bloom all year)
  Words I don't know: stalk

She reads another page, stops, and says, "I don't understand this page. I'm going to read it again." Here she models how one can be confused when reading and how rereading can help clarify. She reads aloud from her note-taking chart, pointing to the words. Then she continues reading the book. "Boy!" she says, "There's a lot to learn on this page! I don't want to copy the whole page. Notice that I only put a few words. I don't write the whole sentence. I'm not trying to rewrite the book, am I?" Here Emelie models what it feels like to be overwhelmed by note taking. She continues, thinking aloud, "I'll put 'page 8' because it has a picture of the inside of a dandelion." She then reviews what she has done, asking the students questions to check their comprehension. She ends the lesson by asking them to tell her one thing that they have learned about note taking. The students comment, "You learn things," "If you don't understand, you can read it again," and "You write down the things that are important." By having the students tell her what they have learned, Emelie makes them think about their learning.

DEAR: Drop Everything and Read

During DEAR time, the students each choose a book to read. Many choose books about dinosaurs to read in pairs or alone. When reading in pairs, they take turns reading aloud and discuss quietly what they are reading. A few read aloud to Emelie, who also reads silently to herself. The DEAR time seems a good way to affirm the value of reading for pleasure. Because they are allowed to choose any of the many books displayed on the classroom shelves, students can read books that are meaningful and interesting to them at a language level that is most comfortable for them.

Writing Workshop

After DEAR time Emelie begins writing workshop with a minilesson on book cover illustrations. She holds up two books, one with a plain cover and one with an interesting-looking cover. She and the students talk about which cover is the most interesting:

Emelie: If you were in the library and saw these books, which one would you pick?

Common Threads of Practice

Students: That one!
Emelie: Why?
Students: It has a nice picture. It looks interesting!
Emelie: My family loves your stories, but they often say, "Don't your students know how to make their books look interesting?" Make your cover look interesting! What are some of the ways that you can make it look interesting?
Students: Lots of colors. Funny pictures.

In this minilesson, Emelie not only teaches her students how to make their books look interesting but points out the importance of writing for an audience.

The students get their writing folders and go to their tables to work on the stories they are writing. The students work at their own language levels: some write three sentences, and some write paragraphs. Some of the children use invented spelling. After students have written their stories, they confer with one another, reading their stories aloud and asking questions of each other (e.g., "What color was the car? Where did they go next?"). These questions encourage students to elaborate on their stories and clarify meaning. Peer conferences encourage independence, responsibility, and cooperation.

Students also confer with Emelie. In a typical student-teacher conference, students first read their stories to Emelie, who then reads the story aloud so that the writer can hear what an audience would hear. She asks questions that enable the writer to understand changes that could be made in order to create a more interesting or understandable story. She then asks if the writer wants to learn where and how to put quotation marks in the story so that it will look like real conversation. The student-teacher conferences allow Emelie to work with students at their language levels. She models good listening, reading back a story to the author and questioning to clarify meaning. She teaches grammar and language use within the context of the student's own writing, tailoring her teaching to the individual student's language use, level, and needs.

Several of the students read their stories to me, and two ask if they can confer with me. One of the children, a native Spanish speaker, has written her story with invented spelling:

> One day I when out side to play with my sister Hat and goced when we wore play we saw a flower the flower was pretty it had pretty color. It had gus two color. It had pink and magenta. And then my sister side a anad littel flower were genu. It was green. When we looked we side the big flower was baid.

When she reads it aloud, she says:

> One day I went outside to play with my sister hide-and-go-seek. When we were playing we saw a flower. The flower was pretty. It had a pretty color. It had just two colors. It had pink and magenta. And then my sister saw another little flower which were growing. It was green. When we looked we saw the big flower was dead.

I notice that the student has circled words that she is having trouble spelling. I ask a few questions about where she wants sentences to begin and end. She puts in periods and capital letters, and then discovers that she needs a verb agreement. "I'm silly!" she says, "It's not 'were' growing. There's only one flower. I should put 'was' growing." By thinking out loud in her conference with me, this student discovers and corrects her grammatical error.

When the 1-hour writing workshop ends, the children are disappointed. There is great excitement when Emelie announces that three students are ready to publish their stories. After the students put their writing folders away, they gather on the carpet in the sharing corner and the first author sits in the author's chair. After she has read her story aloud and shown her illustrations to the class, the students discuss what they liked about her book (e.g., "I liked her pictures!" and "I liked it when the people scared the giant!").

Emelie asks the students what went well in the writing workshop. Students respond with, "I liked it when we were at the illustrating table; we played a joke!" and "I liked it when I did my book," to which Emelie replies, "Tell us the title so that we can look forward to it!" This last remark of Emelie's is just one example of the continual support and encouragement she gives her students throughout the day.

Dialogue Journals

Writing workshop is not the only way that Emelie encourages student writing. She also builds student self-esteem and language development in dialogue journals. Each student writes to Emelie in a journal. Some students write a few words only; others write whole sentences or a page. The length of each piece depends on the student's language proficiency level, just as the length of a student's story in writing workshop depends on the level of his or her language use. Emelie responds in writing to each child. Her notes are enthusiastic, personal, and written so as to be comprehensible and challenging to the child.

Conclusion

I value the time I spent and the things I learned in Emelie Parker's classroom. Every moment of her teaching exemplified how to build student self-esteem, how to build cross-cultural awareness and respect, and how to encourage the use of language in all its forms (reading, listening, speaking, writing, and thinking) across the curriculum.

8

How Do They Learn to Read and Write?

Literacy Instruction in a Refugee Camp

Lauren Hoyt

Preparing Refugees for Elementary Programs (PREP) is an ESL and cultural orientation program operating in the Philippine Refugee Processing Center in Bataan, Philippines. PREP, which has operated since 1986 under the auspices of World Relief Corporation, serves Southeast Asian refugee students being resettled in the United States.

Since the first PREP classes began in April 1987, more than 8,000 students have completed the program. It operates year-round, with new educational cycles beginning every month. Students attend classes 5 days a week for 4 hours a day. Upon graduation PREP student accompany their families to the United States, where most continue their education in public school systems.

Lauren Hoyt, who served as Director of Instruction for PREP, shares the variety of literacy approaches used in the program, including Language Experience, Sustained Silent Reading, the Shared Book Experience, and Process Writing. She also traces the progress of one student, Somlith, as he emerges as a storyteller.

It is May, the height of the dry season in the Philippines. Sweat trickles down my back, but I barely notice as I step from the glare of midmorning sunlight into the classroom's shaded interior. "Good morning, supervisor! How are you?" rises like a chorus from a sea of upturned faces. Small hands reach out to touch me.

A frail girl grabs my hand with surprising vigor and pulls me down to sit on a small wooden chair next to her. She and three other students at her table are absorbed in the process of making a book from newsprint and yellow construction paper. They ardently discuss a caption to go beneath their brightly crayoned illustration. Students at three tables near ours are clustered around similar projects while their teacher, an energetic Filipino, works with a fifth group. I am caught up in their excitement and sense of purpose.

"You read," insists a little boy in an oversized t-shirt. His eyes shine with pride as he lovingly hands me their half-finished book. In three more weeks he and his classmates will complete their eighteen-week educational cycle. They will join a growing number of refugee students in the educational programs across the U.S.A.

"Have we done enough," I wonder, "to prepare them for the challenges that lie ahead?" We have given them a solid start. For children who started with little or no English when they came fifteen weeks ago, who were shy, scared, and confused (many of whom had never been to school), they have come a long way. I glance at the book and then back at these brave new authors. My hope is mirrored in their eyes.

—Journal entry, July 11, 1991

In the 3 years I worked with Preparing Refugees for Elementary Programs (PREP), I never ceased to be amazed by the refugee children's fierce desire to learn. Equally impressive was the PREP teachers' ability to create supportive learning environments and the excitement both teachers and students sustained as they learned about the process of reading and writing from each other. The PREP literacy program was developed under unusual circumstances, and it continues to produce amazing young readers and writers in only 18 weeks.

My involvement with PREP began in 1988 when I moved to the Philippines from Oregon, where I worked as English as a second language (ESL) coordinator and teacher for a public school district. Many of my students were Southeast Asian refugees. Like most people who work with refugee children, I was curious about my students' educational backgrounds and wondered what their schooling had entailed. My curiosity was satisfied by moving to the Philippines, where I eventually learned about refugee training programs from the inside out, particularly the PREP program.

Program Overview

PREP is an elementary program for refugee children aged 6 to 11 1/2 years. English is taught through content areas such as reading, writing,

How Do They Learn to Read and Write?

math, and science, using songs, games, art, drama, and cooking. The students' daily schedules are structured to simulate the U.S. classrooms they will eventually enter.

Students are grouped by age level to facilitate instruction. Six- and 7-year-olds work together because they have similar developmental and social needs. Eight- to 11-year-olds are usually combined to form an additional group. Before entering school, all students are screened for native language literacy, math skills, and ability to read and respond in English. Whenever possible, advanced students are placed in the same class so that they can progress at a faster pace. The teaching load averages 22 students per class. PREP teachers use instructional strategies that allow students to work at their own speed.

When available, an adult refugee is assigned to act as a bilingual assistant for 2 hours a day. Assistants help with small group activities and with the preparation of teaching materials. Because most are not trained teachers, the assistants receive 2 hours of training weekly on such topics as basic educational methods employed in PREP classrooms, second language acquisition, and cultural orientation specific to school.

PREP teachers have found that children learn best when actively involved in the learning process. They therefore employ hands-on activities that require students to begin using the target language before they have fully mastered its form. As they manipulate objects in a science experiment or play a game, students learn the English necessary to participate.

Students are allowed to progress naturally through the initial stages of language acquisition. In the beginning students may employ nonverbal responses, scribble writing, and unconventional spelling. Teachers assess student progress informally through Total Physical Response (Asher, 1977; Krashen & Terrell, 1983), games, writing samples, and dialogue journals. Collaborative projects require students to work together toward a common goal. Less confident students are encouraged to take risks and share what they know with others.

Literacy is taught within a framework that draws heavily on the children's background and experiences in their first language. PREP teachers, who are all Filipinos and second language learners themselves, are sensitive to students' pride in their cultural heritage and first language. They also have high expectations that their students will succeed academically.

The PREP teachers' success with students challenged my notion of what I thought possible. I routinely saw classes of 20–25 beginning students present role plays in English and write simple narratives within the course of the 18-week program.

Approaches to Literacy Instruction

Literacy instruction in PREP is simultaneous with oral language development. Students are encouraged to use their native language and personal history to make connections between what they know and what they are learning.

PREP's literacy program emphasizes instructional approaches that involve students in a common experience that they can discuss as a group. New vocabulary is always introduced within the context of an activity such as singing a song, playing a game, or making pancakes. Language is linked with real situations, either past or present. Students' desire to communicate in the target language with people they know, often the teacher or international volunteers, motivates them to increase their vocabulary and refine their skills in a way that workbooks or repetition drills would not.

PREP teachers use a Language Experience Approach (LEA) (Hamayan, 1987; Holdway, 1979; Nessel & Jones, 1981; Stauffer, 1970) extensively to introduce students to written language. LEA begins with a common experience such as taking a trip to the market, constructing a paper lantern for an upcoming festival, or making popcorn. After the activity the students and teacher reconstruct the sequence of events they have just experienced. New vocabulary and grammatical patterns are introduced. Students then dictate a story about the experience, which the teacher writes on a very large sheet of paper in front of the class. The teacher may sound out key words as they are written, write new words in a contrasting color, or point out conventions such as periods or capital letters. When the story is finished, the class or individual students reread it. Using the students' own language makes the story easier for them to read and is a clear, natural way to help students make the connection between oral language and print.

As the educational cycle progresses, individual students do more of the writing, reading, and retelling. Completed stories are displayed in the classroom for students to reread or refer to when they want to use story words or sentence patterns in their own writing. Students begin to draw on the same language in their dialogue journals (a written conversation between the teacher and student) or use it to play games, perform with puppets, and act out role plays. Language experience writing takes many forms: narratives, poems, letters, and even recipes.

Dialogue journals also play an important role in developing PREP students' literacy skills, and most teachers use them to encourage students to write. The teachers do not correct the dialogue journals; student

How Do They Learn to Read and Write?

errors are viewed as part of the natural learning process. Teachers record and examine errors as indicators of student progress over time. Errors also allow teachers to see how the students are internalizing the instructional input.

As part of their ongoing staff development, PREP teachers reflect in writing on their students' development in English. These teachers have subsequently shared their insights into students' learning in conferences and presentations to other teachers. I draw on the teachers' observations in the remainder of this chapter. In the following excerpt, Gladys Concepcion describes the writing development of one of her 10-year-old Laotian students, Somlith, over an 18-week period (Concepcion & Sumagaysay, 1988).

> Somlith was a quiet boy in class for the first few weeks of school. He is literate in Laotian and used to ask a friend to interpret for him. Since I understood a bit of Laotian, Somlith used to speak to me in his native language. Initially, he knew a basic number of English words and expressions such as "yes," "hello teacher" and "how are you." As his class progressed through the weeks, Somlith became more active and exhibited more confidence. As a part of an ELU [English Language Unit] topic, the second week of the curriculum includes a lesson on classroom objects and locations. Somlith uses pattern writing as he makes use of the vocabulary learned in this particular unit. (See Figure 1, Week 1.)

A week later Somlith's class visited PASS, the camp high school. After the trip, his teacher helped the class write a group story. Later, Somlith used the experience as the basis for a journal entry (see Figure 1, Week 2).

By the sixth week of instruction, Somlith's writing began to reflect his consistent exposure to print. Each day his teacher encouraged her students to read books of their own choosing during Sustained Silent Reading (SSR) time. SSR, another important feature of the PREP approach to literacy development, provides time for students to read or look at books on their own as part of their daily routine. Even those students who cannot read fluently spend 10–15 minutes absorbed in pictures. As the weeks go by, these emerging readers begin to recognize words and to connect them to the illustrations.

In the writing sample in Figure 2, Somlith writes about a topic that is popular with young students everywhere—monsters. His writing shows evidence of the exposure he has had to print materials:

> Here Somlith shows a big change in the development of his writing. In the past he enumerated a sort of word list, writing them in a pattern

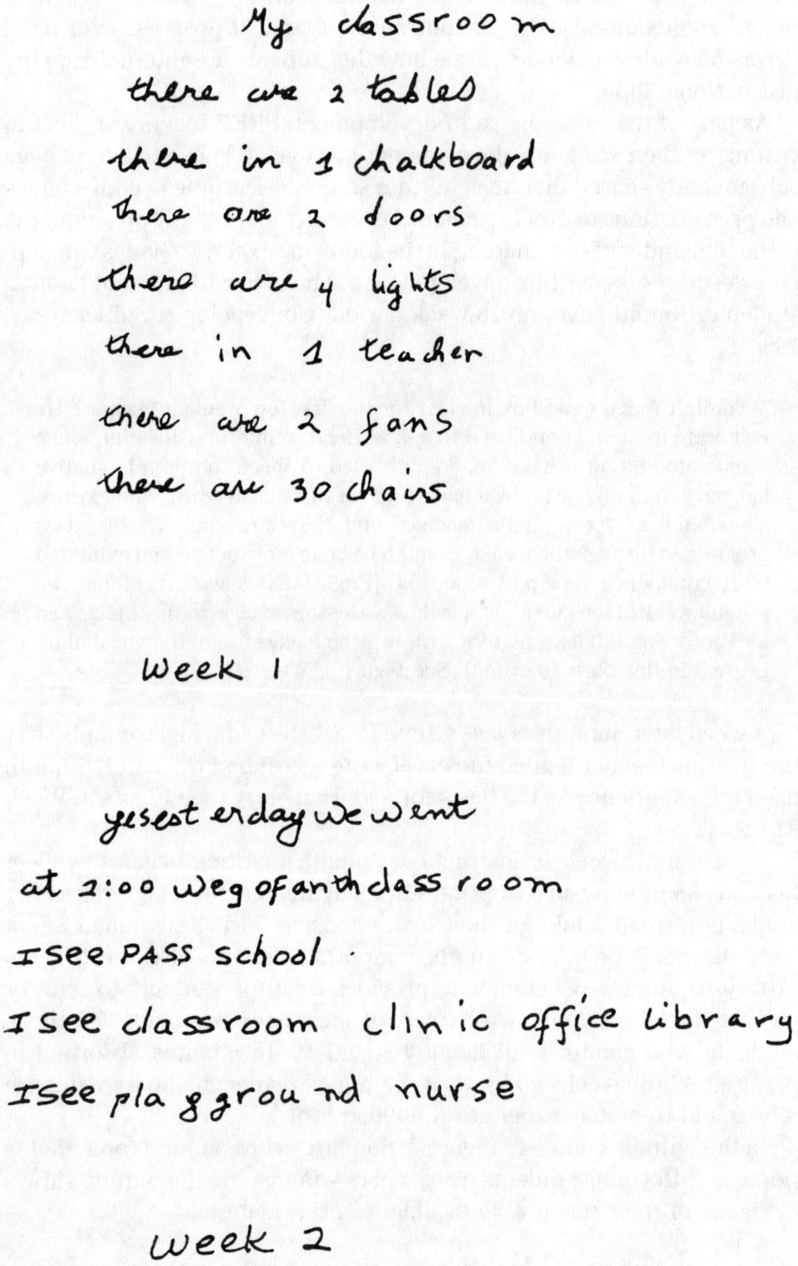

―――――― Common Threads of Practice ――――――

My classroom
there are 2 tables
there in 1 chalkboard
there are 2 doors
there are 4 lights
there in 1 teacher
there are 2 fans
there are 30 chairs

week 1

yesesterday we went
at 2:00 weg of anth classroom
I see PASS school ·
I see classroom clinic office library
I see playground nurse

week 2

Figure 1. Somlith's writing, Weeks 1 and 2.

How Do They Learn to Read and Write?

sentence going from top to bottom. In this particular sample, he demonstrated an understanding of writing left to right. The use of "and" was added to link one phrase to another forming a long sentence which was a reflection of his oral development at the time. (Concepcion & Sumagaysay, 1988)

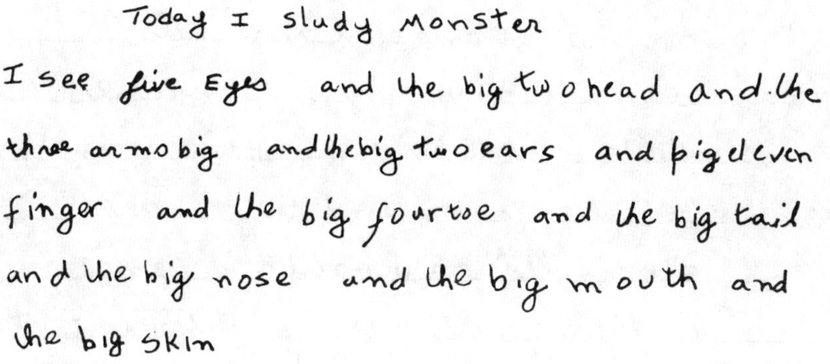

> Today I sludy Monster
> I see five Eyes and the big two head and the three armo big and the big two ears and pig eleven finger and the big fourtoe and the big tail and the big nose and the big mouth and the big skin

Figure 2. Somlith's writing, Week 6.

PREP teachers read to students every day. They use enlarged copies, or Big Books, because they can be seen more easily than library-sized books when the teacher is working with the entire class. This shared book experience (Goodman, 1968, 1986; Smith, 1983) allows teachers to demonstrate the reading process: making predictions based on the illustrations, recognizing words within the printed text, and summarizing or sequencing events. Together students and teacher discuss components of a book such as the author, the title, and the illustrator along with the writing conventions of the language (e.g., capital letters and punctuation). The influence of shared book reading can be seen in the writing sample in Figure 3, written by Somlith in the 11th week of the program. Concepcion and Sumagaysay (1988) write:

> In January, Somlith was already conveying complete thoughts as he was able to internalize concepts. In this piece he also has the concept of a title which was not displayed in his earlier writing. This was something he added after discussing the piece with me. He not only makes use of his nouns and verbs but is also making extensive use of the conjunctions "because" and "and."

By the middle of the 18-week cycle, most teachers begin Process Writing (Clay, 1984; Graves, 1982; Harste, Woodward, & Burke, 1984; Hudelson, 1989) with their students. As the name implies, Process Writ-

Common Threads of Practice

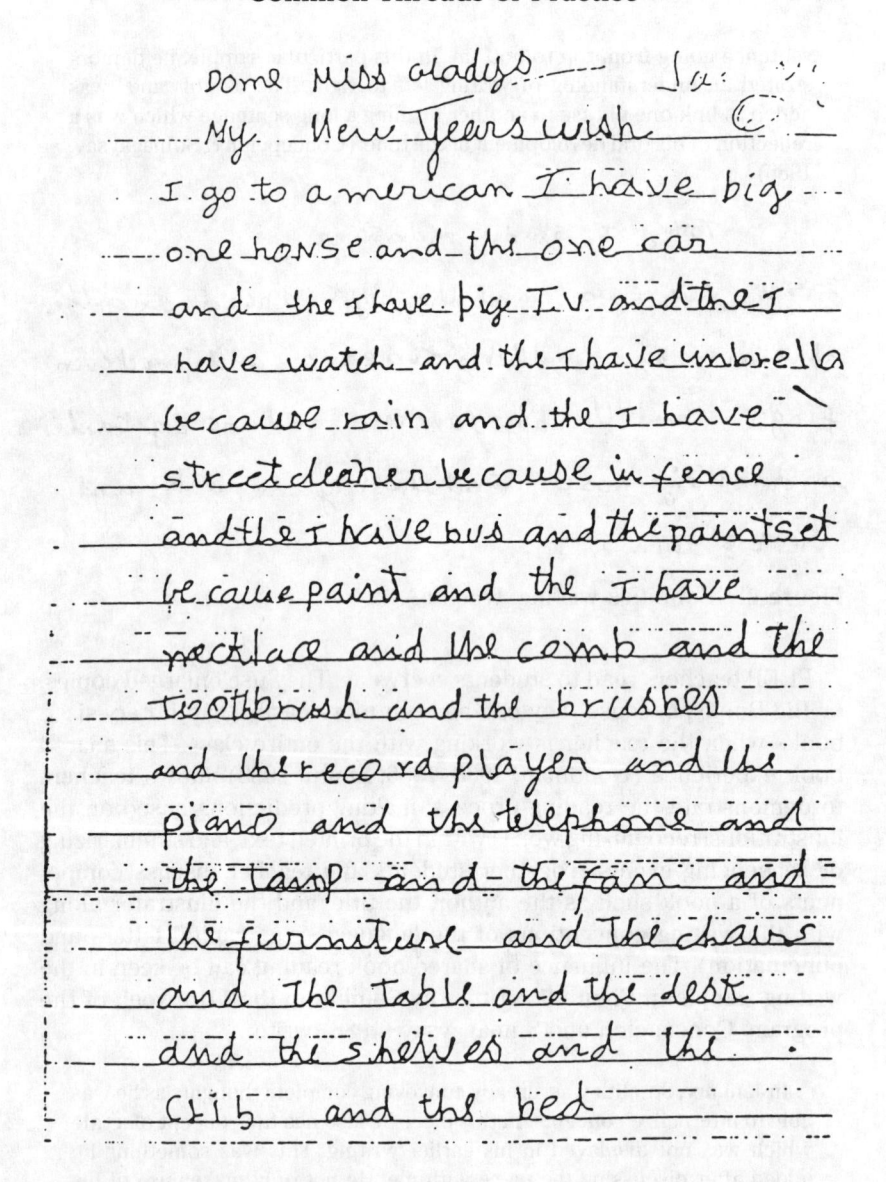

> Dome Miss aladys. — Ja: ...
> My New Years wish
> I go to american I have big
> one house and the one car
> and the I have big T.V. and the I
> have watch and the I have umbrella
> because rain and the I have
> street cleaner because in fence
> and the I have bus and the paint set
> because paint and the I have
> necklace and the comb and the
> toothbrush and the brushes
> and the record player and the
> piano and the telephone and
> the lamp and the fan and
> the furniture and the chairs
> and the table and the desk
> and the shelves and the
> crib and the bed

Figure 3. Somlith's writing, Week 11.

How Do They Learn to Read and Write?

ing leads students through a revision process. Several drafts of a story evolve as students ask peers or the teacher to read through their work and comment on it. These conferences, as they are called, give the teachers a perfect opportunity to use the students' own work to teach the conventions of spelling, grammar, structure, and style. Process Writing provokes great interest among the students because what is being taught relates directly to pieces they have written. Students enjoy reading their finished pieces to the class and getting an honest critique from peers. Finished stories are added to classroom or school libraries so that other students can take them home to share with family and friends.

Students such as Somlith combine language from all these experiences in their reading and writing like the pieces of a puzzle. In commenting on Somlith's final Process Writing project (see Figure 4), the teachers were obviously pleased with his progress, as they observed:

> Towards the end of the cycle, a dramatic shift took place in Somlith's writing. He began to relate a story line and developed it with complete thoughts. There is continuity and development of ideas, such as a beginning and an end. At this point, whereas other students would choose to simply draw and label their drawings, Somlith began to transfer his oral composition into illustrations.
>
> In preparation for this piece, the class had been working together on cooperative writing projects. As a reflection of their Sustained Silent Reading and Big Book reading experiences, they were able to incorporate the elements of character, place and setting into their stories. As I talked to him about his story, Somlith was able to recall the events of a visit he made to the nearby town of Balanga which he was able to weave into his story. (Concepcion & Sumagaysay, 1988)

Conclusion

Somlith's progress was exciting to follow. Through practice and continued exposure to correct forms of the language, Somlith began to recognize when his grammar, syntax, spelling, and pronunciation deviated from conventional forms. His teacher provided models without penalizing him for errors by correcting him. In Process Writing he redrafted his own writing with a critic's eye.

Not all students leave PREP able to write a story such as Somlith's. Most, however, can draw and label pictures, write pattern sentences, and create sequential story lines. In addition, they usually recognize familiar words within a printed text and retell stories using illustrations. Most important, they see themselves as capable readers and writers.

Common Threads of Practice

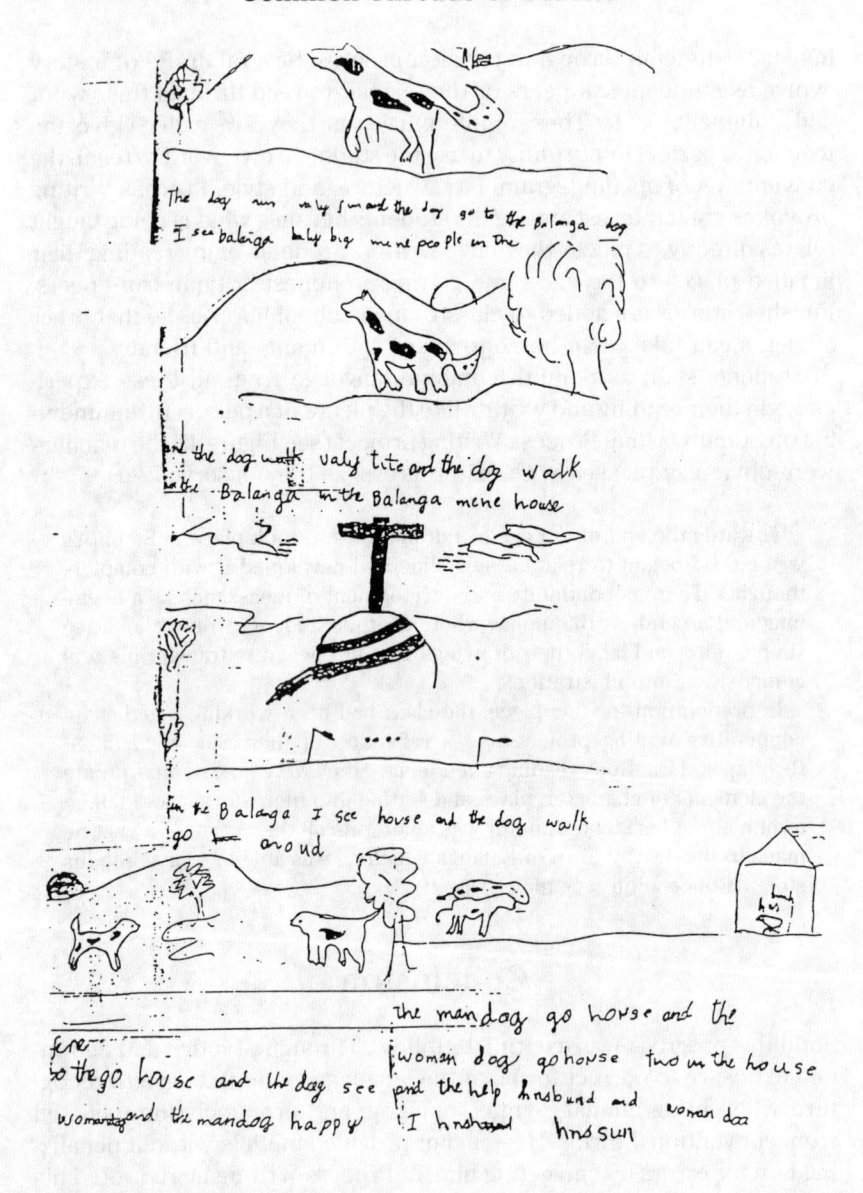

The dog run valy s~~m~~ and the dog go to the Balanga dog
I see balanga baby big mene people in the

and the dog walk valy tite and the dog walk
in the Balanga in the Balanga mene house

in the Balanga I see house and the dog walk
go ~~to~~ aroud

the man dog go house and the
fire
to the go house and the dog see
woman ~~and~~ and the man dog happy
woman dog go house two in the house
and the help husband and
I h~~usband~~ husun   woman dog

Figure 4. Somlith's writing, Week 18.

——— **How Do They Learn to Read and Write?** ———

Like the children I described in my journal that hot summer day, they are excited and proud. They have come a long way. Our challenge as teachers remains: to keep that vision alive in them and in ourselves.

References

Asher, J. (1977). *Learning another language through action.* Los Gatos, CA: Sky Oak Productions.

Clay, M. M. (1984). *What did I write? Beginning writing.* Portsmouth, NH: Heinemann.

Concepcion, G., & Sumagaysay, G. (1988). *An analysis of a PREP student's written work.* Paper presented at the 22nd Annual TESOL Convention, Chicago.

Goodman, K. (1968). *The psycholinguistic nature of the reading process.* Detroit: Wayne State University Press.

Goodman, K. (1986). *What's whole in whole language?* Portsmouth, NH: Heinemann.

Graves, D. H. (1982). *Writing: Teachers and children at work.* Portsmouth, NH: Heinemann.

Hamayan, E. (1987). *Developing literacy in English as a second language (A handbook for teachers of young children).* Arlington Heights, IL: Illinois Resource Center.

Harste, J. C., Woodward, V. A., & Burke, C. L. (1984). *Language stories and literacy.* Oxford: Oxford University Press.

Holdway, D. (1979). *The foundations of literacy.* Portsmouth, NH: Heinemann.

Hudelson, S. (1989). *Write on: Children writing in ESL.* Englewood Cliffs, NJ: Prentice-Hall Regents.

Krashen, S., & Terrell, T. (1983). *The natural approach.* San Francisco: Alemany Press.

Nessel, D., & Jones, M. (1981). *The language experience approach to reading.* New York: Columbia University Press.

Smith, F. (1983). *Essays into literacy.* Exeter, NH: Heinemann.

Stauffer, R. G. (1970). *The language experience approach to the teaching of reading.* New York: Harper & Row.

9

Team Teaching in Second Grade

Don't Pull Out the Kids, Pull In the Teacher

Carlyn Syvanen

The public schools in Portland, Oregon, USA, have begun to experiment with an innovative approach for teaching students of ESL: teaching that teams an ESL teacher with a mainstream classroom teacher. This approach provides a promising new staffing arrangement for schools trying to accommodate increasingly diverse student populations.

Carlyn Syvanen, an administrator in the ESL-Bilingual Program of the Portland Public Schools, describes how Tom (an ESL teacher) and Karen (a second-grade teacher) came to team teach and outlines the advantages of that program design.

One morning on my rounds as a resource teacher, I stepped into the second-grade classroom in Arleta Elementary School in Portland, Oregon. I saw that the daily schedule on the board listed journal writing as the first activity of the day. Children entered the classroom singly or in small groups, hung up their jackets, checked in with the teacher about lunch, and then were directed to get their journals out. I wandered around the room reading journals over the shoulders of the 7-year-olds.

One boy was writing about a trip he had taken to the zoo when he lived in Florida. With the help of a picture dictionary, he was listing all the animals he had seen there. Other children were coloring in a space following the teacher's printed directions: *This is red, blue, green,* and so on. Another was describing the selling of pepperoni sticks to his friends

Team Teaching in Second Grade

and family the day before. Some children had trouble getting started whereas others were done quickly. As they finished, children moved over to the book corner to get a book to read. They sat with their books, alone or in pairs, reading to themselves, to their partners, or to a teacher.

During this period all the children were involved in writing, reading, helping each other, or asking for help. The atmosphere was calm, and everyone knew what he or she was supposed to be doing. It looked like a typical beginning to a day in a typical second-grade classroom in the Portland Public Schools. What made this classroom unusual was that 13 of the children spoke Russian, Vietnamese, Chinese, or Spanish as a first language and were just beginning to learn English, and 11 spoke only English. Except for the Russian-speaking boy, who had arrived just a few days earlier, it was hard to tell who was who. Another unusual feature of the classroom was that in the mornings the English as a second language (ESL) teacher, Tom, team taught with the second-grade teacher, Karen, rather than pull out the ESL students for special instruction.

Why Team Teach?

Tom and Karen began to team teach as the result of several factors: a districtwide movement toward a whole language curriculum, a schoolwide emphasis on meeting the needs of at-risk students, and a large influx of students eligible for ESL-bilingual instructional services.

The first factor leading to team teaching was the district's acceptance of a whole language approach. Karen, the second-grade teacher, was one of the teachers who had greeted the school district's turn toward whole language as progress in moving the curriculum toward how children learn. She felt confident that a whole language approach would help her to provide a learning environment that would benefit all the students. As the number of students who qualified for ESL services increased, she became more aware of how disruptive it was for the children to be pulled out every day for their ESL classes. Even though she knew Tom was an excellent ESL teacher, she began complaining to him that there must be a better way to meet the needs of these children.

The second factor influencing Tom's and Karen's decision to team teach was a schoolwide staff development program focusing on at-risk youth. Arleta Elementary, a K–5 school, is located in a primarily blue-collar, low-income neighborhood in a large urban district. Many of the students are at risk for failure in school as a result of academic, social, or emotional factors. Arleta's students scored in the lower percentiles on districtwide achievement tests. For these reasons the principal and some interested teachers applied for and received a grant earmarked for schools in low-income neighborhoods and with large numbers of underachieving students. These funds were used for staff development, extra planning time in the summer, and release time during the school year. As a result of this staff development program, the teachers began to realize that pull-out programs were disruptive to the classroom and the learners, including those who were having trouble understanding what was happening in the classroom and those who qualified for special help (e.g., ESL; Chapter I, a federally funded program that provides additional instruction in basic skills such as reading and mathematics; or special education, instruction specifically designed for developmentally delayed, physically and emotionally challenged students). The staff began looking for alternatives to these pull-out programs.

The third factor that encouraged Karen and Tom to try team teaching was the fast-growing population of students eligible for ESL and bilingual services. Over the previous 5 years, the percentage of limited-English-proficient students in the school had increased from 7% to 30%—120 students speaking 12 different languages. An ESL-bilingual population of that size was large enough to require an additional staff member and to warrant team-teaching situations at each grade level. Three teachers were thus assigned to the students eligible for the program.

The ESL teachers, the school principal, and an ESL-bilingual program administrator took these three factors into consideration one spring when they sat down to plan for alternatives to a pull-out program. As the group looked at the large numbers of beginning-English-level second-grade students, someone suggested trying a half-day team-teaching approach. Tom immediately thought of Karen's complaints about pull-out and contacted her.

Making Team Teaching Work

By working as a team, Tom and Karen were able to create a classroom environment in which all students could learn. The teachers planned together very carefully so that all students could understand everything that was going on in the classroom. They presented key concepts visually through charts, graphs, models, and pictures, and covered the walls with pictures, charts, directions, models, schedules, and lists.

Two teachers in the classroom provided many opportunities for demonstrations, both planned and spontaneous. When introducing the poem "What Did You Put in Your Pocket?" (de Regniers, 1981), Tom wore an apron with a big plastic pocket and Karen poured milk, chocolate pudding, molasses, ice cream, juice, and sand into it. Everybody learned the poem, even the children who understood very little English.

One day when I observed the classroom, it was Tom's turn to do the calendar. He led the class through the routine of weather, day, date, and counting. The children were sitting on the floor facing the blackboard and, as each concept was talked about, Tom or one of the students pointed to the appropriate picture, number, or symbol or wrote the number on the chart. When Tom asked for possible combinations of numbers that make 25, each child was invited to contribute. The combinations ranged from 24 + 1 to 137 − 112. All correct contributions were accepted, and each child had the opportunity to contribute at his or her own level.

Next, Karen introduced a mathematics lesson on symmetry by cutting a Valentine, a Christmas tree, and a paper doll out of folded paper. She showed that, for an object to be symmetrical, both sides of the center line needed to be exactly the same. Tom, seeing that not all of the students had understood, stepped in to show some negative examples, asking Karen if they were what she meant. She corrected him by showing that when his sample was folded in the middle, the sides were not the same. All the students then went to their seats and cut out various symmetrical shapes, which they glued onto paper. Both teachers moved around the room, observing and assisting as necessary. As students finished this project, they went to Karen in groups of two and three for instruction on how to do two work sheets: one that reinforced their understanding of symmetry and another that challenged them to a higher level of understanding.

All of the students were expected to participate in every activity. Each morning the class held a 20-minute group meeting during which they discussed that day's events, problems, successes, and concerns. By using the Problem-Solving Wheel (see Figure 1), a chart with pictures that illustrate helpful behaviors, all students were invited to identify peers who had been helpful or to share ways they had solved problems that day. Vinh, a non-English-speaking student who had been attempting to solve all his problems with karate kicks and hitting, was able to point to the pictures on the Problem-Solving Wheel to show that on this particular day he had both shared and taken turns, a fact that his classmates corroborated with enthusiasm.

Lessons were structured so that students took responsibility for their learning. The many opportunities for the students to choose and contribute at their own level assured this responsibility. For example, early in the year many of the beginning English speakers copied from lists posted around the room or from simple pattern books during their writing time.

― Common Threads of Practice ―

PROBLEM SOLVING
Try at least 2 of these ideas
when you have a problem

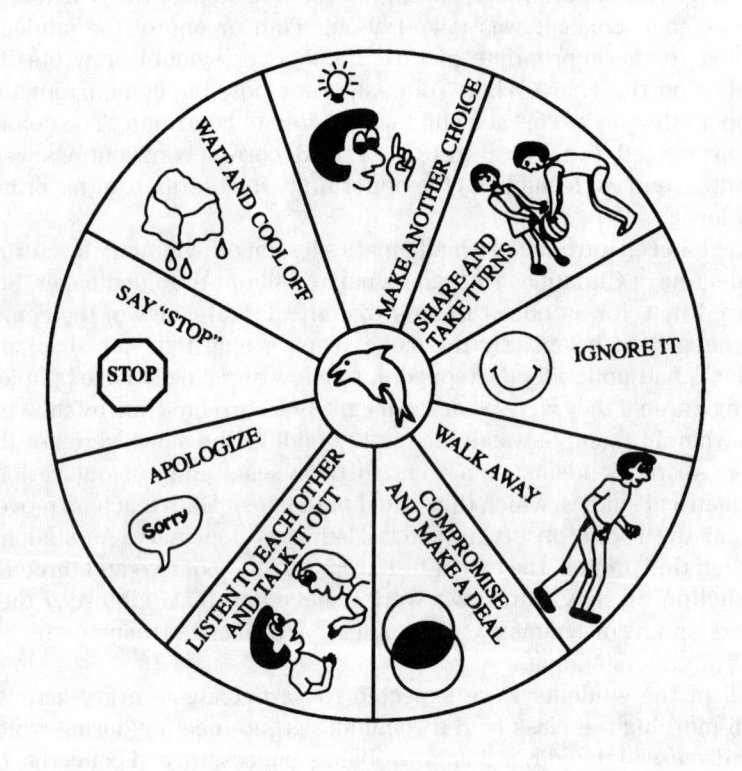

For intimidation,
inappropriate language,
or fighting, tell the teacher
immediately

Figure 1. Problem-solving wheel.

Team Teaching in Second Grade

The idea caught on and soon everyone was copying, even the most proficient writers. Tom and Karen, concerned that the advanced writers were not challenging themselves, brought up their concern in the daily group discussion and talked about the value of copying at certain stages of language acquisition and of doing one's own writing at other stages. Classmates translated the discussion into the ESL students' native languages if necessary. The students then had the opportunity to say whether they needed to copy or to write their own compositions, and each student knew exactly what he or she needed to do. Some explained that they needed both copying and composing because at times they did not know how to write what they wanted to say.

Although students were expected to participate in every class activity, full competence in English was not required. The students participated at their own level of proficiency. This flexibility was most apparent during writing time, when the students took out their writing folders and the teachers circulated around the room helping with questions, comments, and suggestions. During one lesson I observed, students were cutting out magazine pictures, gluing them onto sheets of paper, and writing words or sentences to go with them. Cindy cut out pictures from an old workbook and labeled them with the help of her neighbor: *doll, ball, moon, star*. Kim had four pictures of bears (one walking, one sleeping, one swimming, and one eating) and had written four sentences: "The bear is wakn. The bear is slepn. The bear is simn. The bear is etn." Daniel had filled his page with pictures of dinosaurs and was explaining variations in their sizes, shapes, diets, and other characteristics.

Children learn language when they have the opportunity to use it. This classroom was neither quiet nor dominated by teacher talk. During reading time, a few students read to themselves, but most chose to read to a partner. More proficient readers read to beginning readers and then listened to and helped them. Tom and Karen worked with those who needed the most help. One day Igor and Frank were totally engrossed in a picture dictionary: Igor was calling out the words in Russian while Frank called out the words in English. Two weeks before Frank had protested to Karen, "You mean I have to teach those Russian kids?"

Advantages of Team Teaching

Tom and Karen agreed that, because there were two teachers, they were much better able to organize the classroom. Consequently, they could work more effectively toward their goal of involving *all* students in *all* activities. With two teachers present, they could check that everyone was on task, and while one instructor was involved with whole-group direct instruction, a built-in observer could notice and help those who may not have understood the lesson.

Another advantage of having two teachers in the room was that occasionally Tom could take half the class to the art room, where a video camera was set up. In the making of videos, whether they involved explaining Arleta School rules, dramatizing a story, or reenacting a field trip, each student took an active role: acting, speaking, directing, or holding up cue cards.

For Tom, the major advantage to team teaching was that all students in the classroom felt included. As an experienced ESL teacher he had seen too many situations in which children who did not understand the language of the classroom sat until they had their one opportunity of the day to participate—usually in the 30- or 45-minute pull-out time with their ESL class. In contrast, in this classroom, because the emphasis was on making meaning clear, a great deal of discussion took place in the first language of the students, be it Vietnamese, Spanish, Russian, or Chinese. The bilingual students had the important job of translating. Those who knew only one language were curious to learn how to say things in other languages. As a result, children who the year before had tried to hide the fact that they spoke more than one language were now proudly showing off their abilities. The classroom became a true learning community.

Evidence of community spirit became apparent one day during sharing time. Sergei told the group in his very limited English, with help from Ivan, that someone had taken his snack. As the message was received, Bobby said in a very shocked voice, "I hope no one in this room did that." It was inconceivable to him that a member of their class could do that to anyone else.

A concern at the beginning of the year was that the parents of the English-speaking students would feel that their children were being slowed down because so many children in the class spoke little English. The teachers were pleasantly surprised to find that the only comments they heard from parents were positive. First, parents liked the idea that two teachers were in the room because each child received more attention that way. Second, parents were very enthusiastic about the opportunities that their children had to learn about other languages.

One group of students who received unexpected benefits was the English-speaking students who had been identified in first grade as being at risk for developing academic problems. Those children benefited from the teachers' emphasis on having every child understand what was happening in every lesson. The children also had the opportunity to be seen as experts in at least one area, spoken English, and were able to assist their peers.

The major benefit of team teaching for Tom and Karen was increased collegiality. They felt they both learned a great deal from working with each other and that it would be very difficult to return to working in a classroom alone. One factor contributing to the success of their team teaching, they believed, was the additional time they spent planning together.

Conclusion

Because Tom and Karen enjoyed a successful year of team teaching, they decided to move on to third grade with their class, continuing the approach for a second year. One of the other ESL teachers in the school arranged to team teach in another second grade. The growing number of team-teaching enthusiasts seems to suggest that even more ESL and classroom teachers may be willing to try the approach.

One important element in the success of Tom and Karen's team teaching was that it was a teacher-developed solution to the problem of how to make learning more meaningful for at-risk students. Through the ongoing staff development program on at-risk students, teachers came to realize that pull-out programs were disruptive, not only to the classroom, but to the very students they were designed to help. As teachers began to look for alternative ways to meet the needs of their students, they designed a solution that seemed workable for them—team teaching.

Reference

de Regniers, B. S. (1981). What did you put in your pocket? In *West of the moon* (p. 129). Holt Impressions Series. Toronto: Holt, Rinehart, & Winston.

10

English in Austrian Primary Schools

Maria Felberbauer

Maria Felberbauer discusses English language teaching in the primary schools of Austria, known as English for young learners (EYL). After presenting an overview of one pilot program, known as the LOLLIPOP project, and of the historical context that has shaped language teaching in primary contexts in Austria, she describes the program that has trained all Austrian teachers to become teachers of foreign languages.

Felberbauer is the coordinator of the LOLLIPOP project in Vienna and a professor in the Department of English at Catholic Teachers Training Academy.

I enter the school building shortly after 8 o'clock in the morning. It is a typical primary school with colourful paintings and examples of children's craftsmanship exhibited on the walls. The students and teachers have settled in their classrooms. As I pass each classroom door, I hear the typical sounds connected with teaching: various bits of murmured conversation, laughter, a teacher's high-pitched voice.

Suddenly I hear, "Hello, Sue, how are you?" and then a child's voice sings the answer, "I am fine and what about you?" I stop to listen, hearing the song run on and on, with other names replacing *Sue*. I really shouldn't be surprised because, for almost a decade, English lessons have been compulsory for all third- and fourth-grade students in Austrian primary schools. What does surprise me, however, is that I am standing in front of Class 1B, which contains a group of 6-year-olds.

This first form (or grade) is one of the classes participating in a school initiative launched by the Vienna School Board in the autumn of 1989. The program, which now involves 24 classes of beginners, is known as the LOLLIPOP project. In it, classroom teachers teach English in very short units (approximately 10–20 minutes) every day within the context of the subject matter being taught. The teachers speak in English (instead of German), and the children sing, memorize rhymes, greet each other, and talk about their school supplies, clothes, pets, and toys in English. When children go to the gym, they play games or do exercises using English. Sometimes they do mathematics (simple calculations or just counting or finding certain numbers) in English. Native speakers (e.g., English or American mothers of classmates, foreign students, former nursery or primary teachers) may join them once a week for fun and games.

The class teachers and the advisers working with the children are surprised at the matter-of-fact attitude the children develop toward English as a new way to communicate. Austria is by no means a bilingual country. The influence of English on an Austrian child's world is largely restricted to terms like *jeans*, *t-shirts*, *hamburgers*, and the unavoidable *hot dog* with *ketchup* and *Coke*. Although Austrians do have the option of watching English television programmes, listening to English radio stations, and hearing English used in movies and theatre performances, an Austrian child is unlikely to come into much contact with English.

The children have made good progress in the program, as they pick up sounds, words, and phrases without difficulty, and the teachers are quite happy with it. The LOLLIPOP project allows teachers to decide when and how much English they want to use on any given day. In fact, teachers claim that the only pressure they feel from participating in the project comes from the children: They enjoy English so much that they demand more of it. Parental support for the program is also exceptionally strong, and we anticipate that more classes will participate in the initiative in the future.

A Longstanding Tradition in Austria

Austria has long been a leader in the field of English for young learners (EYL). Thirty years ago most governments in Western Europe started ambitious foreign language programmes in the primary schools. Depending on their location and commercial as well as political interests, the countries chose to teach languages that seemed the most useful to them. For example, the English started with French (e.g., the Nuffield Project); the French began to teach English in some areas; the Germans introduced French in the primary schools in parts of the country that border France and Belgium but opted for English in areas still occupied by U.S. troops. As English was the principal foreign language being taught in Austrian secondary schools at the time, it seemed sensible for Austria to introduce English in the primary schools as well. (In Austria children attend primary school for 4 years [ages 6–10]. They then go on to secondary school [ages 10–15] or grammar school [ages 10–18 or –19].)

The Pilot Projects

In the first experimental period, the ambitious programme ran into three difficulties that almost brought it down: lack of properly trained teachers, no clear-cut methodology for the primary school age group, and not enough public support.

The mechanisms needed to overcome those difficulties took more than 20 years to develop. Teaching foreign languages in all primary classrooms has only recently become an unquestioned and generally accepted practice.

In the first stages of the Austrian programme for EYL, experts were brought into the primary classrooms. These experts, however, were secondary school teachers of English. They were not incompetent as far as their knowledge of English was concerned, but in most cases their methods, although well proven in secondary school, failed miserably with the primary school students.

What does failure in teaching a foreign language to 8- and 9-year-olds mean? Boredom, frustration, and the refusal to communicate in English. In time, these attitudes demoralized the teachers as well as the pupils. The traditional methods of secondary-level foreign language classrooms could not be applied in the primary schools.

Who Should Do the Teaching?

Austrian educational authorities began to recruit primary school teachers who could also teach EYL. These teachers used methodologies appropriate for small children. They knew how much foreign language learning an 8- or 9-year-old pupil was able to cope with, and they worked with students in a way that alleviated boredom and frustration. Their methods, surprisingly, were almost exactly the same as those they had been using to teach subjects other than English. They taught English in a stress-free atmosphere by singing songs, reciting rhymes, playing games, drawing and painting, and doing bits of dialogues that later evolved into role plays.

Teachers and pupils found this way of learning English rather exciting. Teachers were more or less free in their planning of English instructional periods throughout the day. They could place the short units of English wherever they wanted in their schedules, but it soon became apparent that third and fourth graders learned best when they concentrated on learning English for no more than 20–30 minutes at a time.

The teachers also noticed that the speed at which children picked up new language items was nearly equaled by the speed at which they forgot those same words and phrases, especially if long intervals passed between lessons. They realized the children could concentrate longer early in the day. In addition, the teachers began to observe that the children's language-learning capacity seemed to mirror the various stages of cognitive and emotional development through which they passed. Because these classroom teachers were keen observers of their students, they were likely to know at what point their students were ready for certain aspects of the language and would adjust their lesson plans accordingly.

Although most primary school teachers in Austria had studied English in school, their language competence had become rusty over the years. The school boards designed and implemented new courses so that primary school teachers could polish their English pronunciation, intensify their knowledge of words and phrases used in everyday situations, refresh their knowledge of basic grammar, and be trained in methods of foreign language teaching. Over the years, these training programs have helped to create a rather unusual situation for those teaching English in non-English-speaking countries: In Austria, every primary school teacher is now also a teacher of foreign languages.

Training Primary School Teachers to Teach English

Today, primary school teachers are trained at teacher-training colleges. They enter teacher-training programmes after passing their final exams at a variety of preparatory contexts: grammar school, a secondary commercial school, a secondary school of home economics or kindergarten training, or any other institution that offers a comprehensive final exam called the *Matura*. After passing this examination, the students are usually 18 or 19 years old and can enroll at a university, a teacher-training college, the military academy, an academy of music or arts, or any number of professional training colleges.

When students come to the teacher-training college, they have studied English for 8 or 9 years (in addition to 2 years of EYL in primary school). Most of the students have taken written and oral examinations in English. Quite a few have also studied 4 years of French or another foreign language, and approximately 50% of the students have studied Latin for 4–6 years. The intensive foreign language education that students receive throughout their school careers makes it feasible for Austrian primary teachers to become EYL teachers as well.

At the teacher-training colleges, all students are required to take English for 1 or 2 hours a week per semester (six semesters in all). In addition to this basic language training, the students complete special coursework that prepares them to teach EYL. The coursework includes the study of:

- the psycholinguistic development of young children, including native and second language development
- English classroom vocabulary
- methodology for teaching in the primary language classroom, including using songs, rhymes, language games, storytelling, role plays, jazz chants, and content-based English
- materials development.

The students practise these teaching techniques in small groups. In addition, they teach a number of English lessons in primary classes.

A Little Learning Goes a Long Way

In some countries, early language learning failed because there simply was too much of it. Expectations were high, but the results lagged far behind. For example, when Great Britain's National Foundation for Educational Research evaluated the results of teaching French in the primary schools, it found that the time and effort spent to teach French to 8-year-olds was out of proportion to the amount the students learned. The effect of this report could be felt all over Europe. In Austria the number of schools participating in the experimental stage of EYL dropped significantly in the early 1970s.

More recently, however, a new approach to primary methodology in general has laid the groundwork for a resurgence of interest in teaching of foreign languages in the primary schools. By 1983, 1 hour of English (or French), called Preparatory Foreign Language, had been integrated into the Austrian primary school curriculum.

The Austrian national curriculum now includes one lesson (50 minutes) per week of foreign language teaching in the third and fourth grades. In more than 90% of the cases the language taught is English, although in some schools French is compulsory, with English usually offered on a voluntary basis. Bilingual schools in ethnic minority areas follow the same curriculum. Syllabi for English and French in primary school have been developed.

Teachers are encouraged to split the 50-minute weekly English lesson into two or more units to make the most of children's shorter attention spans. All children participate in the language course. A number of books have been written, and many teaching materials have been developed to assist teachers with the course. Parents are informed about the aims of foreign language teaching in the primary schools. The English curricula of the secondary schools have also been modified to ensure continuity of learning across grade levels.

What Happens in the Classroom?

Because the Austrian educational authorities believe that children's introduction to foreign language learning should be stress free, there is no formal assessment, and, consequently, no grade in English in the annual report. The authorities feel that the first contact with a new language should help to develop a positive attitude toward the target culture and open the children's horizons toward other ethnic groups.

Language teaching in the primary schools emphasizes the development of listening and speaking skills, including listening comprehension exercises, talking about oneself, asking and answering questions of immediate interest to the children, initiating short dialogues in the context of the child's realm of experiences, and practicing pronunciation, intonation, and sound discrimination. Learning English is connected with enjoyable activities like singing songs; learning rhymes and chants; playing games like dominoes, Bingo™, and Happy Families™; and doing short role plays based on real life.

Reading and writing (including spelling) in English are only of minor importance at this level. The written exercises in the fourth class are kept to a minimum (filling in blanks, solving puzzles, doing transfer exercises, filling in grids, and combining parts of sentences). Short texts for reading (e.g., programmes, posters, advertisements, postcards, and greeting cards) are as authentic as possible. Although there are no formal tests, teachers informally track the progress of and difficulties encountered by each student.

Teachers employ great methodological expertise to keep motivation at a very high level. Native speakers are invited into the classrooms; tourists from all over the world and an increasing number of members of United Nations organisations in the country ensure a ready supply of English-language models.

How to Keep an Old Tradition Young

Recently many new ideas have come into the field of EYL. Interesting methods like storytelling, English across the curriculum, activity-based language teaching, and topic-centred approaches have led to an integrative methodology in the field. Although most of these practices have come from the area of English as a second language rather than from English as a foreign language, Austrian primary school teachers have been able to modify and use them. Teachers are encouraged to participate in in-service training courses arranged by the local Pedagogical Institutes, and some primary teachers even attend special courses at English universities or teacher-training institutions.

Contacts with other European countries interested in introducing English into primary school settings are frequent and promising. The educational authorities of former Eastern Bloc countries whose more traditional methods of language teaching are undergoing rapid changes have recently approached Austrian experts in the field for advice. This role keeps us thinking about the approach we use. However, whenever visitors come into our primary classrooms and watch an English lesson, they are most impressed by one fact: The young pupils who are learning English there are having great fun.

11

Teaching English to Children in China

Bi Qing

Generally speaking, Chinese students do not begin to learn English until they are 12 years old. Now that China enjoys greater international contact, however, the need for people who know foreign languages has increased, and attention has shifted to teaching English to young children.

In this chapter Bi Qing, a kindergarten teacher-researcher, describes her English program in an experimental school in one of China's largest cities, Shenzhen. English instruction at that level focuses on listening and speaking, and relies heavily on games, music, dance, and drama.

I am a staff member of Shenzhen Experimental School, which consists of an experimental kindergarten, an elementary school, and a middle school. Most of the students at our school live in the neighborhood surrounding the school. My job, and that of other teachers in the school, is to try out new teaching methods, content, and administrative systems, and then to share our experiences with other educators throughout the municipality, province, and country. English teaching is a key issue for researchers, and the staff places a great deal of emphasis on revising teaching materials.

Kindergarten Section

I am in charge of researching English teaching in the kindergarten section of Shenzhen Experimental School. The 270 children in the section attend the school for 8 hours every day. Apart from time spent on games and outdoor activities, the children have classes in subjects such as language, mathematics, social studies, nature study, and music. English teaching is scheduled for 20–25 minutes after breakfast, during the time for academic development. Every child has the chance to take English classes three times a week.

The children are divided into three groups according to age: an older group (aged 5–7), a middle group (aged 4–5), and a younger group (aged 3–4). There are three classes in each group, for a total of nine classes in the section, each with about 30 children. I usually teach children from all three groups each day.

Theoretical Framework

As a newly developed city, Shenzhen is full of immigrants. The children therefore encounter many dialects and are ready to be stimulated by a new language. My teaching benefits greatly from their readiness. Because I majored in early childhood education in college, my teaching is particularly influenced by the psychological processes of children's language learning. Another influence on my teaching is the Japanese educator Dai Ibuka, who hypothesized that the best time to learn a foreign language is while acquiring one's native language—from birth to age 6. According to Dai Ibuka, all children have the potential to develop more than two language centers in their brain, and if they receive only native language stimulation, their other language centers will gradually degenerate. Dai Ibuka also believes that if children begin to learn a second language after the native language center has been established, it will be very difficult for their brains to absorb a second language. This theory is reflected in my teaching goals and methods.

Teaching Goals

My goal is to provide a variety of activities and a relaxed and healthy environment so that children can actively learn spoken English (and develop an interest in learning more English). By focusing on spoken English, I can lay a solid foundation for reading and writing in English in the future.

The great difference between teaching English in kindergarten and in primary or middle school is that English classes are not compulsory. Also, because kindergarten activities focus on music, dance, acting, and

Teaching English to Children in China

cognitive development, the children think that they are just playing when they are actually learning a new language. In fact, my English teaching is a series of learning activities, not formal lessons. The activities are grounded in the children's interests and ability to imitate, and are designed to promote the overall development of the children's minds and bodies. I do not judge the success of the learning activities by looking at how many words or sentences the children have memorized, but rather by observing how well they speak and understand English.

Teaching Methods

Listening and Speaking

In kindergarten I focus on training the children to understand, listen, and speak rather than on teaching letters and spelling words. A great deal of language input and many opportunities to practice make the language more familiar and accessible. In this way students acquire correct pronunciation and intonation, and receive good grounding for their study of written English in primary school.

When I introduce a new word or sentence, I do not write it on the blackboard for the children to read but say the word while showing them the item. For example, when I say the word *cat*, I show the children a toy cat or a picture of a cat while imitating its sound and actions. In this way I make a direct connection between the word and the concept. For commands such as *get up* or *sit down*, I indicate with gestures that the children are to get up and sit down, again linking meaning with actions.

If the children are learning a song, I do not teach them the song line by line or explain the meaning word by word. Instead, I let them enjoy it first and then use drama and dance to demonstrate the meaning to them. Sometimes the children cannot help but join in and dance! When we begin to sing the song, I read them the key words several times, and they soon understand. The reason the children can easily master a whole song is that they have been able to focus first on understanding what the song is about. Listening and understanding are at the core of speaking, and from this I draw the conclusion that listening, understanding, and speaking are at the core of reading and writing.

Conceptual Development

Based on my understanding of how children learn, I select vocabulary that the children are interested in. Much of the content I teach relates to animals, feelings, body parts, everyday objects, foods, numbers, vehicles, professions, names of places, and adjectives and verbs used in everyday life.

The content is presented in lessons that progress from simple to complex and from easy to difficult, targeting the varying needs of the three age groups. I plan units of study that are grounded in core vocabulary and consist of a sequence of activities (e.g., drills, songs, short plays, and games). Usually we complete one unit each month. Below are lesson plans for two units I have developed.

Animal Unit

Vocabulary:	*Cat, duck, pig, cow, chick, sheep, bear, monkey, rabbit, elephant*
Drill:	Q: What's this (that)?
	A: It's a cow (duck, pig, etc.).
	A: It's an elephant (alligator, octopus, etc.).
Songs:	"Old McDonald Had a Farm"
	"Going to the Zoo"
Short Plays:	"The Wolf and the Sheep"
	"Little Rabbit's Birthday"
Game:	Guess which animal does this action and makes this sound.

Number Unit

Vocabulary:	*One, two, three, four, five, six, seven, eight, nine, ten, eleven, twelve*, etc.
Drill:	Q: How many days are there in a week?
	A: There are seven.
	Q: How many people are there in your family?
	A: There are five (etc.).
	Q: How old are you?
	A: I'm four (five, six, etc.)
	Q: What time is it now?
	A: It's nine (twelve, etc.)
Rhymes:	"One, two, three, climb a tree.
	Four, five, six, pick up sticks.
	Seven, eight, nine, everything is fine.
	Ten, eleven, twelve, help yourself."
Musical Game:	"Ten Little Indians"
Short Play:	"Snow White and the Seven Dwarfs"

Based on my understanding of children's cognitive development, I teach content in direct and simplified ways. I rely heavily on body language, including facial expressions and hand gestures. In this way I demonstrate the features of animals and imitate their sounds and movements. Sometimes I ask the children to generate their own actions in order to stimulate their imaginations and creativity. At suitable times I also use pictures, slides, puppets, and costumes. Thus I incorporate both listening and speaking into activities in which the children use their whole bodies to improve their memories.

Teaching Through Drama

I often develop special plays and skits and let the children take parts. For example, when I teach language that requires making a request, such as *May I have a pen?*, I play a shopkeeper and the children play customers who ask for certain items. When teaching greetings, I write short plays such as "Little Rabbit's Birthday." In this play the children make believe they are little animals visiting the rabbit's home. Before going into the rabbit's house, they greet each other and introduce themselves. Children show extraordinary interest in short plays, which give them opportunities to reveal their language abilities. For example, after watching a puppet show several times, they can vividly retell it.

I often divide the children into small groups and ask each group to play one part while I play another. After a while the groups change parts. Finally I ask individual children to act in front of us all. Drama holds the children's interest, and instead of being asked to focus on and repeat isolated words or sentences, they are learning language in context. When the children leave kindergarten, they are able to act out at least four plays that I have either written or rewritten. The most popular plays are "Snow White," "The Wolf and the Sheep," and "The Hare and the Tortoise."

Teaching Through Games and Songs

Games help me maintain the children's interest while they practice the language. The telephone game, for example, is excellent for developing pronunciation skills. The children sit in lines and whisper a word to the person next to them, who then passes on the message. The process is repeated until the message has been passed on down the line. We also have contests to see who can be the quickest one to find the right color or who can put the five senses in their correct places on a picture of a face. These games motivate the children to try very hard.

English songs are indispensable elements in my teaching. After learning about the body and the five sense organs, we sing "Head, Shoulders, Knees, and Toes," and when learning musical instruments, I teach them "I Am a Fine Musician." Singing English songs helps the children learn how to pronounce English words correctly. Singing songs at the beginning of a class can help them to concentrate and harness their energy. I have also incorporated some songs into group dances and musicals.

My goal as an English teacher is to integrate learning and play. The children sing and dance one moment, and imitate and play the next. They are always actively involved in learning.

Snowball Teaching

Because children have short memory spans, I pay great attention to review and seldom spend the entire time with new content. The sequence of events for a class goes something like this:

1. songs to capture the children's interest—new content
2. games to review content introduced earlier—familiar content
3. musical play—new content

I liken this approach to teaching to a snowball; the old is stabilized while the new is expanded on.

Final Thoughts

Many people believe that young children have an advantage in learning language, especially spoken language. In my experience the program at the Shenzhen Experimental School enhances the children's ability to learn English. In fact, we are now comparing the English language development of students who went through our program with that of students who did not. We are optimistic about the outcomes of this research.

12

Primary Education and Language Teaching in Botswana

Lydia Nyati Ramahobo and Janet Ramsay Orr

The rapid expansion of access to education in Botswana outpaces the speed with which schools can be built or teachers trained. Luckily, the subtropical climate of the southern African nation accommodates classes held under thorn trees and classroom lighting provided by the sun, as rainfall rarely exceeds 25 inches a year, particularly in the western portion of the country—the Kalahari desert.

The characters in this description of English teaching in the primary schools of Botswana are composites of teachers and children the authors have encountered during their research and teaching activities in Botswana. The authors were part of the Primary Education Improvement Project, a joint effort of Ohio University, the U.S. Agency for International Development, and the Government of Botswana. Lydia Nyati Ramahobo is a lecturer in the Department of Primary Education at the University of Botswana. Janet Ramsay Orr is on leave from her position as ESL coordinator for Fairfax County Public Schools, Virginia, USA.

After a decade of independence (1966–1976) from Great Britain, education in Botswana left much to be desired. Most literate parents preferred to send their children to neighboring South Africa for schooling, despite its apartheid policies. The government of Botswana began to acknowledge the shortcomings of its inherited education policies and set up a National Commission on Education (NCE) to evaluate the entire educational system.

The NCE report set the stage for educational reform. It stated that education should be a means to achieve democracy, development, self-reliance, and unity, which together form the national philosophy of *kagisano* (social harmony) (National Commission on Education, 1977).

Based on the findings of the NCE, the development of new education policy began in earnest, centering on providing:

1. universal primary education by abolishing school fees at primary levels (school fees have now been abolished at all levels, including the university level)
2. access to 9 years of basic education by restructuring schools from 7 years of primary, 3 years of junior secondary, and 2 years of senior secondary education to a 6:3:3 configuration.

Language in Education

In addition to these two sweeping changes, the NCE also recommended a substantial change to existing policies on language use in the schools. Although the national language of Botswana, Setswana, is the home language of 90% of the population, English is the official language of government and business. Before the publication of the NCE report, all instruction was conducted in English. The NCE recommended that initial years of schooling be conducted in Setswana, with English taught as a school subject during that time. In Standards (grades) 4 and 5, when children are approximately 9–11 years old, English was to be introduced as the medium of instruction in content classes, with instruction in Setswana continuing as a separate subject. To graduate from primary school, however, students would have to pass the Primary School Leaving Exam, which would test all subjects (except Setswana) in English.

Changing the language policy in the schools so significantly presented many challenges. Because not much was written in Setswana, scores of new textbooks needed to be written and produced, the curriculum had to be revamped, and most important, teachers needed to be trained and retrained.

Because the preparation of adequate numbers of trained primary teachers had become such an urgent need, the Primary Education Improvement Project (PEIP), a contract between the U.S. Agency for International Development and Ohio University, established the Department of Primary Education at the University of Botswana. PEIP took three steps toward the reform of primary education. First, a bachelor's degree program in primary education was designed to train two types of personnel: lecturers to teach in the primary teacher training colleges, and education officers to supervise schools around the country. The need for lecturers in primary education was especially critical. At that time the majority of lecturers were former secondary school teachers, most of whom had not been in a primary school since they themselves were students. Consequently, they trained primary school teachers using secondary school methodology—chalk and talk.

Next, in-service education programs were expanded. Additional teacher centers were created throughout the country to provide support and additional training to practicing teachers. Finally, specialized diploma and advanced degree programs were developed and implemented to prepare teachers to assume leadership roles in primary schools or in the Ministry of Education.

Education Reform in Action: The Observations of One Education Officer

John Diele, our student at the University of Botswana, came to us as an experienced Standard 6 teacher who had grown up in one of the larger villages in the eastern part of Botswana. After earning a bachelor's degree in primary education, he was posted to a remote area of Botswana as an education officer.

In his post John spends most of his time traveling the dusty back roads of the bush visiting schools. He may spend 3 or 4 days at one school, advising individual teachers, giving workshops for the whole staff, clarifying the implementation of the syllabus, or advising the headmaster on administrative issues. John shared with us the following vignettes from his first year as an education officer. His observations of English teaching in primary schools, particularly in Standards 4 and 5, when English is not just taught as a subject but is used as a medium of instruction, illustrate the struggle to implement the new language policy, moving children from one language to another.

Tsayang School

Mrs. Tsheko, the headmistress of the school, stresses the need for English. She expects her teachers and their students to speak English both inside and outside the classroom. Mrs. Tsheko says that English is important for her school because it is the language used on the examinations, and good results on the examinations make her school look good. On John's visit to the school, however, he finds that the way language is used varies considerably from the official policy expressed by Mrs. Tsheko.

Mr. Pule's Standard 5 Class

Kabo bashfully moves over on the bench in the back of Mr. Pule's Standard 5 class so that I can sit down. The benches are squeezed in between the long, slanted student desks. There are more than 40 students in this class. Someone must not be here today, or else this space would be taken.

Mr. Pule begins the English lesson by telling his students to open their English books to page 25 and to look at the story at the top of the page. Then he begins reading:

Mr. Pule: This is a story about Thabo and Dudu. Who can tell us what the fourth word was?
Moses: Sorry.
Mr. Pule: It was not sorry. You have to learn to memorize words, *lo tshwanetse go itse gore ke ne ke bitsa jang.* [You should know the order in which I called these words.] *Ke mang yoo gakologelwang* number four? [Who remembers what the fourth word was?] *Ga gona ope yoo e gakologelwang?* [Nobody?]

After Mr. Pule finishes the story, he instructs the students to take out their English exercise books and complete the first exercise. Students copy six sentences, filling in words left blank in the sentences. Mr. Pule continues the English lesson by asking the students to draw a picture of their village and to write four sentences in English about it. He tells the students that their stories should be similar to the one he has just read about Thabo and Dudu in their village.

Thamie Ramalefe and Yshepo Rakola, two of Mr. Pule's students, produced the stories in Figures 1 and 2. What is interesting about these two stories and the pictures that accompany them is the way the children use English and Setswana. True to Mr. Pule's instructions, the children have written sentences in English that describe their village. Within the drawings, however, is evidence of how English and Setswana interact on a daily basis outside the school. In Thamie's drawing (Figure 1) the word *Milk* is written on a truck and the words *Letamo dam* label what appears to be a reservoir. As English is the language of business and

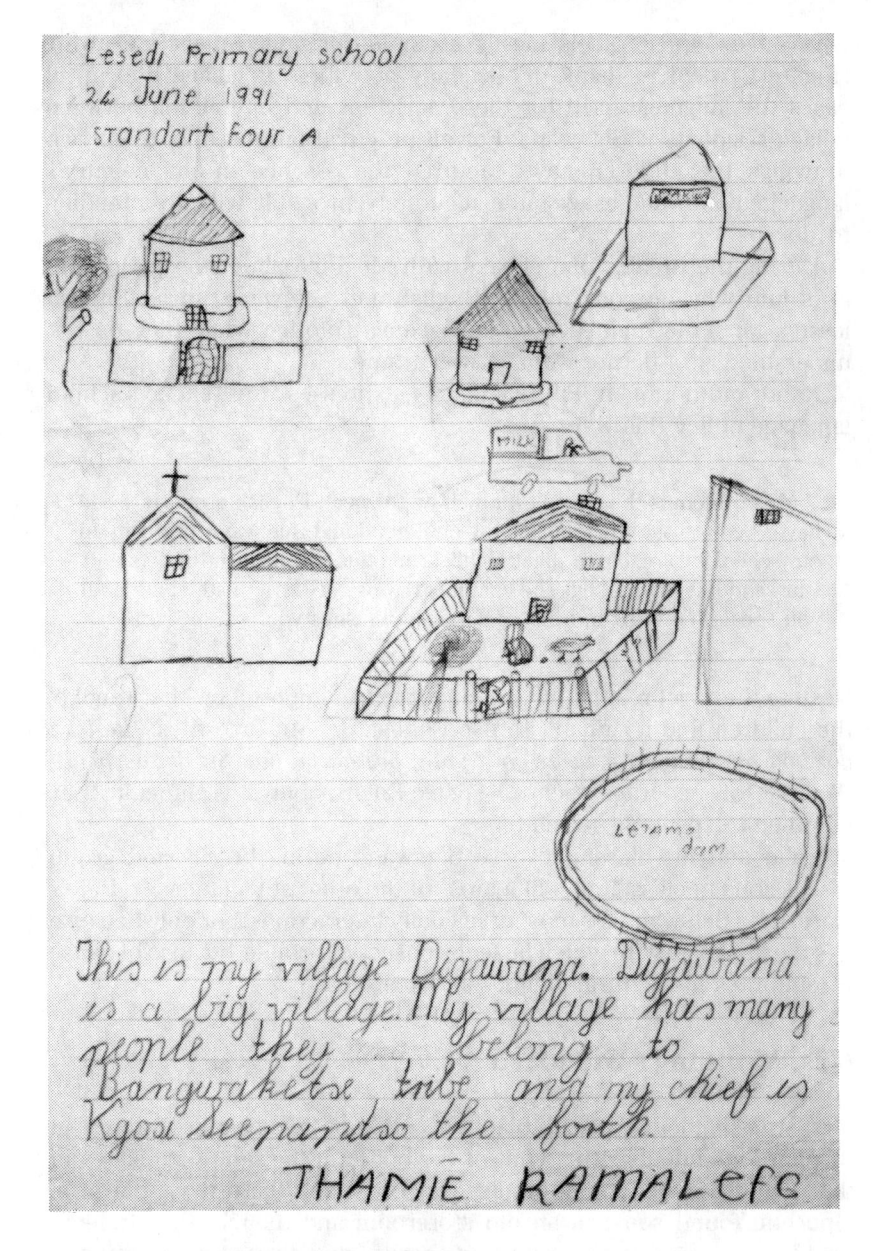

Figure 1. Story by Thamie Ramalefe.

government, these labels hardly seems surprising. Yshepo's drawing (Figure 2) depicts many of the daily activities of village life; in all cases the language used for these activities and interaction between village residents is Setswana. For all practical purposes, in these two drawings the children have captured the essence of the country's language policy and usage quite accurately, probably without intending to do so.

During the break, John speaks with Mr. Pule about the lesson. He asks him why he code mixes (English and Setswana) in an English lesson. Mr. Pule replies, "I do so because I notice when they do not understand, so I do not want to waste time."

Kabo, another of Mr. Pule's students, expresses Mrs. Tsheko's school language policy this way:

> My problem is that I don't know how to speak English properly. I had never been to the town during my childhood and this was a problem. In our school we are told to speak English, and this has made me understand. Our school is interesting. The headmistress is very strict with children. If you speak Setswana in front of her, she punishes you.

Despite the strict regulations on language use imposed by Mrs. Tsheko, the children find it difficult to use English. As Mr. Pule says, *"Re leka gore ba bue Sekgowa, mme go a pala, banna ba bua Setswana hela."* [We try to encourage them to speak English but it is difficult; they continue to speak Setswana.]

Kabo and his classmates use Setswana during breaks and group discussions in class. Kabo, like most of the other students in Mr. Pule's class, uses Setswana for most of his daily interactions, not only because it is the language with which he feels most comfortable, but also because it reinforces his cultural identity as Motswana.

Mrs. Mpusang's Standard 4 Class

Mrs. Mpusang leans a small blackboard against the base of a tree. Ten Standard 4 students sit in front of the board in the sand with slates in their hands. Slates are rarely used in Botswana these days, but Mrs. Mpusang found some in an old storeroom and thought the students could use them as slates or writing boards when they weren't sitting at desks. The students copy each multiplication problem as Mrs. Mpusang puts it up on the blackboard. As the students finish working the problem, they hold it up for Mrs. Mpusang's approval. The teacher acknowledges

– Primary Education and Language Teaching in Botswana –

Figure 2. Story by Yshepo Rakola.

Common Threads of Practice

each correct answer in Setswana and asks one student to look at his problem again.

Two other groups of 10 students are working independently. Each group has a tin can full of bottle caps. A student in each group pours the bottle caps into the sand and begins distributing them to the others in the group. Moving over to one of the groups, Mrs. Mpusang draws two circles in the sand and places nine bottle caps in each circle. She writes $2 \times 9 = \underline{}$ on one student's slate, then begins counting the bottle caps in the two circles in English. When she reaches the total, she writes 18 next to the problem on the slate. In Setswana, she instructs the students to work together to make up their own problems, using the bottle caps and writing the problems on their slates. Students check each other's problems by holding up their slates for approval from the group's self-appointed teacher.

John is very pleased with the instructional strategies he observes being used in the lesson but wonders why Mrs. Mpusang uses English for all the numbers in the math lesson and Setswana for giving instructions to the students. During the break he asks her about it. She says, "When English is the medium of instruction, the children become less active participants. I wanted them to learn how to multiply properly." John agrees that it is important to have full participation by the students. Mrs. Mpusang, like Mr. Pule, is coping with the intricacies of using English in an academic setting.

Trends in Language Use

After observing classes at the Tsayang Primary School for 2 weeks, John has noted some trends in the way English and Setswana are used. His observations of Mr. Pule's and Mrs. Mpusang's lessons reveal that teachers of children at the critical transition stage from Setswana to English tend to code mix in certain predictable ways. The code mixing underscores the difficult task that teachers face: striking a balance between carrying out the school's (and the nation's) education policy and ensuring that students understand and learn the content of their lessons.

In addition, John suspects that classroom language use illustrates the difficulties teachers themselves have in maintaining an all-English instructional environment. Mr. Pule, for example, tries to stick to the expected language of instruction; he is most successful when that language is Setswana. When English is the expected medium of instruction, he uses both languages in the lesson.

But teachers do not give up. They continue to insist that children use

English as much as possible. One day, in Mr. Pule's social studies lesson, John hears him say:

Mr. Pule: OK, let's continue, what are rights, human rights? [long silence]
Mr. Pule: What are rights? You do not know human rights?
Students: *Gare itse Ka Sekgowa.* [We don't know it in English.]
Mr. Pule: *Ete!* You don't know in English?
Students: Yes, sir.
Mr. Pule: Oh! *Ee, mme lo tshwanetse go itse nnetane tsa teng.* [Yes, but you must know those things.] Let's talk about rights, what's rights? What are rights?

Although teachers want students to respond in English, Kabo and his Standard 5 classmates feel more comfortable responding in Setswana. When students are given a chance to use Setswana, the lesson comes alive and they contribute to discussions. For example, following a Standard 5 social studies lesson broadcast over the radio in English, Mr. Pule reviews the vocabulary from the lesson in Setswana. He follows this review with a discussion about tools used in the "olden days." During the review and discussion, Kabo and his classmates volunteer comments and are relaxed and laughing. They understand the lesson and easily express their thoughts on the topic.

Finally, John observes that teachers are often unaware (or do not acknowledge) how much their own ability to speak English affects the way they teach. Although teachers often state that their reason for switching from English to Setswana is that the children do not understand English, John suspects that they fail to see that they often switch into Setswana because they themselves are having difficulty.

Education policy demands that teachers insist on the use of English in the classroom despite their own difficulties in communicating clearly in English. As a result, the teachers' instructions are sometimes unclear and provide a poor English language model. Nevertheless, teachers are often the only model students have (especially in rural areas), so students' acquisition of English (and their ability to pass examinations) depends on teachers' ability to strike a balance between learning the language when lessons are taught in English and learning the content of those lessons.

The Future

As the population in Botswana continues to climb at a rapid rate, so does the demand for primary schools and teachers. With more than 100 new primary schools built between 1989 and 1991, new graduates of the four teacher-training colleges are in high demand. Today, only 15% of the primary school teachers are untrained, compared with 40% 10 years ago; by 1996–1997 there will likely be enough trained teachers that no primary school will have to hire untrained teachers. Headmasters, however, still complain of teacher shortages and must hire teachers who have completed junior secondary school (9 years of education), but who have not received the additional 2 years of training to become a teacher.

The standard for entry into the teacher-training programs has also risen progressively. At one time the entry requirement was completion of 7 years of formal education. With each successive set of applications, however, a higher level of basic education combined with experience as an untrained teacher has become the norm. In fact, a new pilot program at one of the teacher-training colleges requires teacher candidates to be high school graduates (that is, to have passed "O"-level examinations) before their application for training will be accepted and extends the period of study from 2 years to 3 years. These additional years of schooling are quite important for another reason. Because the teacher-training programs are conducted in English, they provide teachers-in-training with more exposure and practice in the language. As the teachers' English language skills increase with additional education, so will the quality of primary education.

Conclusion

Botswana, like many other countries, is struggling with education reform. Although the country has adopted a bold education policy designed to be more responsive to children's need to learn both their native language and English, John's observations suggest that implementation of such a policy is a tricky proposition, particularly for the teachers who carry out the policy on a daily basis. Teachers watch their students struggle to understand and learn English knowing that the children's educational futures depend on their ability to function in an all-English instructional environment. They, in turn, struggle with their own ability to teach exclusively in English.

Some people suggest that Botswana should return to its former policy of using English exclusively; others suggest that native-language instruction should be extended into all grades of school. For now, however, Botswana, its teachers, and its students continue in their struggle to make the current policy work, despite the numerous constraints on their ability to carry it out.

Acknowledgments

We thank Jeannie Haseley and Max Evans for their guidance on this paper.

Reference

National Commission on Education. (1977). *Education for kagisano* (Vols. 1 & 2). Gaborone: Government of Botswana.

13

A Tale of Two Cultures

At Home in the German School Washington

Donna Stassen

Donna Stassen, an ESOL teacher at the German School Washington (Deutsche Schule), describes the English program in the school's elementary section (Grundschule). The students are primarily German speakers whose parents have been assigned to work in the United States. Situated in Potomac, Maryland, USA, the school lies close to Washington, DC.

The school and its staff try to help youngsters become bilingual and bicultural through the English program by integrating language instruction with a selection of content that reflects the culture of the students' host country, the United States. The program helps youngsters develop a sense of their own place in the world community.

The German School Washington (GSW) is a private school in the state of Maryland that is subsidized by the German government. The school ultimately offers the *Abitur* (secondary school leaving certificate) after 13 years of study (excluding nursery school and kindergarten), as well as the high school diploma after 12 years (excluding nursery school and kindergarten). The elementary school, which operates within the larger school, consists of grades 1–4. The majority of the teaching staff is German, and all classes, except English, are taught in German.

Many children come to the school because their parents, who work for the German government, the German military, the World Bank, or German businesses, are on temporary assignment in the United States.

A Tale of Two Cultures

In addition, some children from U.S. families, some from bilingual-bicultural families in which one parent is an American, and some from other countries attend the school. These children are often described as *third-culture* children; that is, they spend part or all of their preadult lives residing and being educated out of their country of citizenship. They come to feel most at home in a third culture created by relating parts of their two cultures to each other (Useem, 1976). The school is located in a U.S. suburb, which provides a broad environment with abundant opportunities to nurture the children's fluency in English. This environment is vitally important for the children from U.S. families who will remain in the United States and provides a golden opportunity for children who will be moving on to another German school after a few years to acquire English.

In the program at the GSW students can maintain their academic development as well as literacy and fluency in the German language. The program is designed to enable students who return to Germany to continue their school work at grade level. The language of instruction in all classes, including mathematics, social studies, science, sports, music, and art, is German. English class is the exception. In the first grade students receive 2 hours of English instruction a week; in second grade, 3 hours a week; and in third and fourth grades, 5 hours a week.

Feeling the constraints of the limited time for English instruction, the English teachers at the GSW have searched for strategies to help make the most of the hours they have. Of course, the cultural environment outside the school is a great help, as well as the numbers of children from bicultural families and those whose mother tongue is English. These two factors provide abundant real-life opportunities for many of the children to test and use their English.

The after-school and weekend activities in which children and their families participate are obviously important in determining how proficient the children become in English. Some families interact almost exclusively with the German community (e.g., school friends, embassy personnel, business colleagues). Although the U.S. cultural scene is at least peripherally a part of their experience, they are less a part of it. Even though their homes are scattered throughout the greater Washington area, including suburbs in Maryland and Virginia, children from such families play with each other outside school. Other children manage to make friends with U.S. children in their neighborhoods and enjoy being integrated into a larger group outside the school community. A good number are members of local swimming clubs and soccer teams, and look forward to being of an age to play basketball.

Program Design and Philosophy

The school has two sections, or homerooms, at each grade level, and children remain in the same section for the entire 4 years, taking all their subjects in the same homeroom group. With limited time and resources, we must teach English in homeroom groups composed of recently arrived students, native speakers of English, and others who have been in the United States anywhere from 1 to 4 years. Each week we offer 2 hours of concentrated English for speakers of other languages (ESOL) for both third-and fourth-grade newcomers, but the remaining 3 of the 5 weekly hours are spent within the grade-level group. As necessity is the mother of invention, I have learned much from meeting the challenges this situation presents and, in fact, have discovered some advantages in mainstreaming ESOL children in a context that fosters bilingualism and biculturalism.

The Program in Action

One of the first things a visitor to the GSW might notice is the friendliness of the children, demonstrated by cheerful greetings on the playground, in the corridors, and in classrooms. Soon thereafter the visitor will probably note quite a range of hellos: from *good morning, hello, hi,* and *yo, dude!* or *gimme five!* to *guten Morgen, 'Tag, gruss Gott,* and *hallo!* English greetings usually come from the children who have been in the school for at least some months and from those newcomers who reveal a special pride in beginning to feel at home in their new environment. Many of these greetings are for me, their English teacher, whereas the German greetings are usually directed to my colleagues who teach their classes in German. The ways children address and communicate with each other in various situations throughout the school day sometimes stem directly from the setup of the program. Sometimes, though, social and cultural factors determine which language the students use (e.g., whether they are making friends with a newcomer who knows no English or talking about seeing the movie *Home Alone*).

Content-Based Language Teaching

As so much of the children's learning takes place in German, and as we are committed to promoting bilingualism, the children must explore a broad range of topics in English. We therefore emphasize content-based

A Tale of Two Cultures

language teaching, an approach that we find very helpful in meeting the needs of a multilevel group because children with different levels of language ability can explore a topic and participate in lessons.

Our starting point for planning is to identify the topic to be explored and aspects of the topic that might be of particular interest to a given class. In the past my classes have explored the animal kingdom (e.g., dinosaurs, turtles, crabs, snakes, sharks, and whales); natural catastrophes (e.g., tornadoes, floods, and lightning storms); developments in technology (e.g., robots, video books, organ transplants); and living in today's world (being in the capital of the United States, the unification of East and West Germany, and the war in the Persian Gulf). We have also celebrated U.S. national holidays and heroes and learned about the role of Native Americans and African Americans in the United States.

Indispensable to our program is each child's subscription to *Weekly Reader*, a weekly newspaper for school children that is published in separate editions for each grade level. Reading through the newspaper together each week stimulates and supplements the study of high-interest topics. It provides us with a broad common ground for learning activities and is one of the key materials in the organization of multilevel learning activities.

Grouping . . .

Once I know what topic we will be working on, I begin to identify and develop activities that involve all the children at their varying levels of language ability. After choosing an article with a high interest value, such as one on television commercials ("Fewer Ads on TV," 1991; see Figure 1), I rewrite it for my newcomers, simplifying sentence structure, content, organization, and vocabulary. The modified version includes underlined vocabulary, questions on content, and suggested learning extension activities. While most of the children read the newspaper independently, I turn my attention to the ESOL group. I give them their newspaper and the modified article, which I introduce through discussion, and use the pictures in the newspaper or other objects or pictures I bring in to make the topic comprehensible. Then I read the article aloud and students volunteer to reread it. We practice the vocabulary, discuss the content questions, which some can begin to answer in writing, and clarify how to do the activities.

As I finish with the newcomers, I turn my attention to the others in the class. Often I notice that the children who are at an intermediate to high-intermediate level have been listening in and gaining a little extra help, whereas those who have English as a mother tongue or are truly

— Common Threads of Practice —

Fewer Ads on Children's TV

How many TV commercials do you see in one day? 5? 25? 100? Many children see about 100 commercials or ads a day. Experts say that by the time most children are 18 years old, they will have seen more than 200,000 TV commercials.

That may change. A new law has been passed that limits the number of ads on children's TV shows.

The new law was passed last fall, but it will take several months for the changes to show up on TV. The law will limit the number of commercials that can be shown in an hour. On weekend shows, the law will allow 10 1/2 minutes of ads in an hour. On weekday shows, it will allow 12 minutes of ads in an hour. Before the law was passed, there were no limits.

The new law may help improve the shows available for children to watch. It requires TV stations to show more programs that help teach children as well as entertain them.

According to studies, children between the ages of 4 and 12 have a lot of their own money to spend. The whole group spends about 9 billion dollars a year! All the advertisers want children to buy their products.

Commercials make toys, games, clothes, and food look good. The ads are hard for children to resist. Experts say that many children can't tell the difference between the ads and the programs. Some little children don't even understand what an ad is. They don't realize that the ads are only trying to sell them things.

Vocabulary Box

advertiser—one who presents products for sale
commercials—ads; announcements trying to sell products

Figure 1. Article on advertisements on children's television. From "Fewer Ads on Children's TV," 1991, January 4, *Weekly Reader* (Edition 4), 72(13), pp. 1–2. Copyright © 1991 by Weekly Reader Corporation. Reprinted by permission.

bilingual have finished the entire newspaper and are quite impatient to begin the discussion. Questioning and discussion help me to determine which children have read carefully; sometimes we must reread and find sentences in the articles that have led to certain opinions or conclusions.

As the ESOL children are finishing their work, I send them to the school library where they are helped to find something they will enjoy reading on their own. Quite frequently, Bjoern, a fourth grader who shows promise as a researcher, has returned with a book on the topic we have been discussing in class and has drawn some of his more advanced classmates into further discussion.

Another topic, introduced through the newspaper, that aroused fascination was snakes, and my more advanced pupils, in particular, began collecting material from the public library for reports. In the same cooperative spirit demonstrated by Bjoern, Ben brought in a stack of books and included two in his collection that he rightly considered to be of special value for his ESOL classmates.

. . . And Regrouping

Cooperative learning projects have also worked quite well with my students, particularly at the fourth-grade level. Using this strategy, I have extended a multilevel lesson taken from an article on the drought in California and organized groups to complete a questionnaire on how different people would be affected by the drought and what they could do about it. The exercise demanded that the children think and work together. Each group had one ESOL pupil as well as more advanced students. One person led the discussion, one wrote, one read the results to the class, and the entire group helped the ESOL pupil determine what kind of poster to make to help people realize that they should conserve water. As the children all speak German, they can help each other through that language, but only when really necessary.

Common Interests

The use of the *Weekly Reader* has been particularly helpful in creating a natural language environment. Topics discussed in school are very often of interest at home as well, and we hear that discussion spills over from the classroom to the dinner table. Furthermore, topics are timely, and frequently what has been reported in the children's newspaper is in the daily newspaper as well. We can therefore extend a lesson with clippings, particularly for more advanced fourth graders. Interested pupils can add to their information while extending vocabulary and reading skills.

Some topics draw in visitors and materials from the community. Children have brought turtles, crabs, a snake in formaldehyde, a snakeskin, shark's teeth, and a whale adoption certificate. Their contributions are invaluable in creating an exchange of information and ideas among the children and furthers development of their language.

In the second grade the exchange of ideas helps us in some serious catching up. As we do not begin systematic instruction in reading English in the first grade, we have to take advantage of the 3 hours of English instruction available to us to do so in the second grade. With the help of the school librarian I have attempted to create a community of readers in this class. Although we work from a basal reader in Grades 2–4, I encourage those who are able to read widely in trade books. At the start of the school year, the children who can already read English independently go to the library for a part of one period a week to choose a book. A book report form gives them the opportunity to keep some notes about each book they have read, but the real excitement for them comes in going to the library together and recommending books to each other. As their excitement has grown, so has the motivation of the others in the class. One by one they have asked to be allowed to be a part of this library visit. In several cases, the growth of motivation has been *the* big step in learning to read English.

A variation of Show and Tell, in which children bring to class things relevant to the topic being explored, is also important in my first-grade class. One day Aaron, a first grader for whom a relative had adopted a whale named Crystal, brought his adoption certificate and a book on whales and gave an informative oral report on the whale adoption program. Sometimes it works the other way around, with Show and Tell stimulating interest in a topic. The visit of a turtle named Geeker, brought to class by a fourth grader, Sarah, motivated an in-depth study of "The Hare and the Tortoise." Follow-up study included the reading of a couple of versions of the story, one a very modern one called *Harry and Shellburt* (van Woerkom, 1977), and a movie version. Finally, the children made cardboard turtles that they raced on strings—a slow and tedious process that brought home the "slow but steady wins" point of the story.

Putting It in Writing

Interesting writing projects are invariably effective with our students on many levels. Challenged with a given topic, whether a creative topic or one that involves organizing thoughts around a problem or question, our

A Tale of Two Cultures

pupils respond enthusiastically to the opportunity to communicate their own ideas. For advanced students, the challenge is in presenting their best work. Thinking, planning, rereading, and rewriting are goals that I put before the most advanced. Kristina, a fourth grader, will return to Germany in the fall after having been in the United States for 4 years. She has a special facility for language and clear thinking. On the problem of pollution she wrote the following:

> Pollution
>
> Our earth is dying. Why? You guessed it! The answer is pollution. Trees, plants and animals are dying because of it. We need plants and trees to live because they produce oxygen from harmful carbon dioxide. So if plants die, animals die, if animals die, people die. So actually, we're killing ourselves. Even if we don't, we're going to end up living on dumps. You can help prevent pollution by recycling, cutting up 6-pack rings, using your bike more, etc. Sometimes it's a sacrifice, but it's worth it, right?

Susanne, a classmate of Kristina's, has been here for less than a year but is already able to write short paragraphs independently in response to pictures accompanying news stories:

> Alaska
>
> In Alaska is much snow. A man is going fishing in the snow. An elk is pulling the sled. The man wants to eat the fish. It is so cold in the snow.

Those who have spelling difficulties do cooperative revision activities; a child who can spell well helps another find and correct mistakes. Those who are no longer at a beginning level in English may write their own stories or paragraphs, though they may need help in spelling correctly.

ESOL pupils may dictate to me in English, if they are able; otherwise they dictate in German and I write for them in English. I encourage absolute beginners to render their ideas in picture form, and I help them explain in English. The payoff for all students comes when the children share their work with each other. All have something to contribute, and stories and ideas from all levels are interesting.

A writing project was the springboard for Denis, a third grader, to realize that after 1 year he didn't belong in the extra ESOL classes anymore. He already used basic greetings and had frequently spoken English during the previous year, but what loosened his tongue for good was the experience of having center stage reading a story that he had dictated in English. Now in the fourth grade, he loves to tackle writing projects but struggles with spelling, as this first draft on inadequate fire security indicates:

No Fire Sikjuriti

Once tehr wos a Hotel fire, only on 2 flors were Sprinklers and no emergency Exits wer in the Hotel. 12 people wer ded and 600 injured. It was the werst fire in mans History.

[No Fire Security

Once there was a hotel fire, only on 2 floors were sprinklers and no emergency exits were in the hotel. 12 people were dead and 600 injured. It was the worst fire in man's history.]

In the Works

The basal readers used in Grades 2–4 and the spelling books used in Grades 3 and 4 ensure that the children are mastering the basics of English literacy. Although we feel that many features of our program work well, we continue to look for ways to improve. At this writing we have already decided to include a spelling book to develop phonics skills in second grade and phase out the basal reader in favor of even more extensive use of trade books. We contemplate the introduction of a new series of basal readers for third and fourth grades that will include a greater number of topics grounded in U.S. history and culture at the third-grade level and international topics at the fourth-grade level.

Conclusion

Teaching English at the German School Washington is a challenge and an opportunity. The emphasis on German language and curriculum places limitations on instructional time for English, yet we feel we achieve a high level of motivation and meaningful learning through relevant instruction that orients the children to their immediate environment and beyond.

Grouping and cooperative learning help us to make all the children a part of the learning community in the classroom. We hope that our English instruction in the context of the GSW will help them to feel at home in two languages and two cultures and, perhaps, eventually see a role for themselves in an international context. We feel we are beginning to meet this challenge when, as our students leave for the day, some of us hear *'Wiedersehen!* or *Tschuss!* while others hear *Bye-bye!* or *See ya' tomorrow!*

References

Fewer ads on children's TV. (1991, January 4). *Weekly Reader,* Edition 4, *72,* 1-2.

Useem, R. H. (1976, September–October). Third culture kids. *Today's Education,* pp. 103-105.

van Woerkom, D. (1977). *Harry and Shellburt.* New York: Macmillan.

14

Teaching English in Estonia

Using Reading and Writing Process Methods to Teach English as a Foreign Language

Emma Wood Rous

Emma Wood Rous, an English teacher at Oyster River High School in Durham, New Hampshire, USA, describes a 10-day sojourn in Estonia dedicated to introducing EFL students to a process approach to reading and writing. Rous took with her suitcases full of picture books and novels from which students selected reading materials. Often the books they selected had great personal meaning for them. While reading, the students wrote about the books in journals and discussed them in class.

When Rous taught in Estonia, the country was struggling to become an independent nation separate from the Soviet Union. Rous suggests that a process approach to teaching her students enabled many of them to deal with the sociopolitical changes in which they were engulfed.

Emma, you must stay here or we all come with you to America! With you the week was interesting. It's bad that this week so quickly ended. All was as a wonderful fairy tale. —Dora

It was really wonderful English. We have never had such before. We are blown away! —Riina

I think that this week when we were here together with you, this was just like. I haven't been in paradise but I think that this was a paradise on earth. —Virge

You brought together with you a draught of fresh water. —Astrid

Such was the response to 10 of my most enjoyable and rewarding days as an English teacher, days spent not in my regular high school classroom but in an English as a foreign language (EFL) classroom in the small seaside town of Haapsalu, Estonia.

In 1989, an Estonian Bridges for Peace delegate observed individualized reading and writing process instruction in New Hampshire schools and was inspired to introduce the methods in Estonia. The following spring two other English teachers and I were invited to Estonia for 10 days to teach English. Our intention was to test our belief that the same reading-writing process approach that succeeded with American students could motivate students learning EFL. Could intensive reading and writing in English, with grammar instruction used to reinforce comprehension and expression rather than being the primary focus of instruction, be an effective tool for teaching the language? Must students master the rules of a language before they can express themselves in it, or will the effort to communicate foster language mastery?

Features of My English Teaching

In my classroom in New Hampshire, I emphasize the interrelatedness of reading and writing, the belief that reading leads to better writing and that the process of writing makes more sensitive readers. Because students are most motivated to learn when they read and write about subjects that are personally relevant, my students write about their hopes, dreams, fears, and best and worst experiences.

The process of developing each piece of writing receives as much attention as the final product. Students share their writing, and read and discuss published writing in a continuing exploration of what makes writing effective. They learn the mechanics of writing and develop style as a response to their need to express their thoughts. Such relevance seems just as important to students studying a nonnative language as to those writing in their native language. Even native speakers must continue to learn how to make their language work for them, and it is the desire to communicate that enables learning to occur in a first or, presumably, a subsequent language.

Language Teaching in Estonia

The timing for introducing new methods of instruction in Estonia, especially English instruction, was ideal. When we arrived in Estonia, the possibility of travel to the West was still an exciting new prospect for Estonian citizens. Estonia was in the throes of separating from the Soviet Union, and the study of English was a political act. Estonians had been required to learn Russian, but Russians in Estonia (40–50% of the population) attended separate schools and, at least in the past, did not study Estonian. With independence now a reality, language continues to represent national identity and autonomy, and Estonian is now required in such fields as public security and health. For Estonians, to study English is to reject the language of oppression and to embrace what one of our Estonian students, Virge, called "the language of the whole world."

Language teaching in Estonia has been influenced by the traditional Soviet curriculum, which placed great emphasis on memorization and recitation. Textbooks are centrally planned and distributed. One teacher lamented that students might do well on examinations but still not be fluent speakers or writers. She described the experience of a colleague who had emphasized spontaneous conversation over the prescribed curriculum, only to be criticized when his students received lower exam scores. A typical English textbook includes grammar exercises, dialogues for memorization, and reading excerpts from classics by such authors as Henry Wadsworth Longfellow and Jack London, or stories of brave Soviet youth who sacrificed self for country. Teachers' attempts to supplement these materials are thwarted by the lack of copy machines and the scarcity of paperbacks in English. The Russians set up language specialty schools in central cities, but none exist in outlying areas such as Haapsalu. There, English is taught in 40-minute periods twice a week, starting in the fourth form when students are 8 to 9 years of age. Students who choose a humanities specialization study foreign languages four times a week in the upper forms. English is at least the third and sometimes the fourth language studied, after Estonian, Russian, and Finnish.

In addition to these problems, there are not enough teachers to fill the current demand for English, especially now that better-paying opportunities exist for English speakers in the growing private sector. The training of English teachers has been hampered in the past by lack of contact with native English speakers, the reason we were invited into Estonian classrooms. We were the first native English speakers that many of our students had encountered.

Reading and Writing Process Instruction in Haapsalu

In Haapsalu we were assigned to a middle school and a high school. I taught two groups of 12 students in two 3-hour sessions each day. Four students quoted in this article came from the ninth form of 13- and 14-year-olds (Annika, Jane, Liina, and Maarika); the remaining students were 16- and 17-year-olds about to graduate from high school.

Our plan for the students was fairly simple. They would choose books they found personally relevant (we came armed with suitcases full of paperbacks), keep reading response logs, and share books orally in class. They would also generate ideas for writing based on personal feelings and experiences using a process of brainstorming, draft writing, reading to peers, editing, and rewriting final pieces.

The same teaching methods were successful with both age groups, the only difference being that the younger students were less fluent in English. Consequently, the same exercises took more time and the students wrote less, at least initially. Because of their lesser exposure to English, the younger students had more limited vocabularies and often chose shorter books to read. The two examples of extensive written revisions that follow (Liina's and Annika's) were from younger students and demonstrate how well the process of writing and rewriting from personal experience can work for this age group. With more time, similar work could be expected from more of the younger students.

What Students Wrote About

Students wrote about being teenagers and described their fears, dreams for the future, and best and worst experiences. When I asked them to tell me about themselves, the students, who had never been asked to write about personal issues, even in Estonian, poured out their hearts. Because they had the double motivation of wanting to learn English and communicate feelings and ideas they cared deeply about, they worked hard to make English speak for them. The dictionary pages flew, they came to me and each other with questions, and they wrote some exceptionally powerful pieces. All the student writing is quoted here as originally written; not every piece was edited and rewritten. Students wrote sad stories (e.g., about the divorce of parents or the death of a friend), but they wrote happy, upbeat pieces as well, particularly about travel and music. A few members of the class had taken part in a student exchange in Sweden that permanently changed their world perspectives. Merle wrote:

> In Sweden, I met a lot of interesting people from different countries. We talked straight about drugs, racism, sex, AIDS, suicide, alcoholism. Because it is evident that young from all over the world have almost the same problems. We discussed ecology and peace and everything else

which excited us. We reached a conclusion that the most important thing is to try to make peace. Many people feel more despair than hope when they think of the future. Our technology can kill everything that lives. Every person can help make a peace.

As Merle discovered in Sweden, young people around the world share universal dreams and fears. My students hoped for an education, work, travel, marriage, a home, and children. Liina wrote, "My main dream is to learn art at the art university. Of course I hope to become rich and go hiking!" And Jane wrote:

> One of my hopes is to have a good education and go to learn in a university. After university I want to find work so that I will feel content. Always work goes in life—doesn't who ever work, he doesn't eat. One of my dreams is to get a wonderful cottage, where I can do housework. The cottage must be in a romantic place and be by the sea. I want to have a good husband too . . . . My largest dream is to have a baby. I want to be a good mother. I want to have a good and beautiful life.

Their fears have the same universal ring. "I fear death, war, exams," wrote Merle. Maarika worried about the environment and wrote, "I'm worrying about our country. Because our country is very small. And very defiled. We don't know which is our country in the future. Have we clear sky and water?"

How the Writing Evolved

Several of the student pieces quoted above developed from an exercise calling for each student to list the 21 best and 17 worst things that ever happened to them, choose one, and list all the words that come to mind when they think of that event. Such a brainstorming method is valuable for helping students generate ideas before worrying about form or grammar. From these notes, students wrote first drafts, then shared their pieces with each other and with me. They seemed to find reading their papers to each other both unusual and very helpful. Dora wrote, "I very like our learn system. I don't see my mistakes but when I read Eve's story I find her mistakes and then my mistakes too." The students agreed that they learned from each others' mistakes and from their sentence structure, vocabulary, idioms, and expressions.

My comments on students' writing came in two stages. First, I posed questions and ideas to help them clarify and expand the writing to make the pieces as vivid and real as possible. Finally, I edited for errors. Here

Teaching English in Estonia

is how this process worked with Liina's description of a summer rock festival. She first wrote a short description on an index card:

> One of most important events in my life was the rock festival, Rock Summer '89. I get striking feeling and I understand what I like summer and mad young people. There was many good music and I enjoyed it.

After general instructions to the class to use as much detail as possible and to try to make readers feel present at the events described, she wrote the following draft:

> One of the most important events in my teenager years was rock festival, Rock Summer '89. Music has important part of my life. "Rock Summer" took part in Tallinn in June and lasted for three days. From morning to evening, for three days on end, I heard good music.
>
> There were the best groups from Estonia and many good and interesting groups from Sweden, North Ireland, Finland, United Kingdom, USA. There was music, from country to punk rock.
>
> Concerts took place on two stages—one big and one small. There wasn't any pause in music.
>
> From that big snarl of music I got a striking feeling. I understood—I love summer, music, hamburgers, and crazy young people.
>
> After the end of the concert I had to go home by the train. Next morning I went to the excursion to Lithuania. And I couldn't understand—was it real?

This draft showed a real effort to further define and convey that "striking feeling" Liina had at the concert, and I complimented her on her descriptions. I also read a few phrases aloud to the class as examples of vivid description. I made some suggestions regarding grammar (articles, verb tenses) and structure (keeping setting details together), and wrote some questions in her journal: "Did you go with friends? Did you like some groups more than others? Can you describe more details about the crowd, or one of the music groups?" Here is the final draft:

> One of the most important events in my teenage years was the rock festival, "Rock Summer '89." Music has always been an important part of my life.
>
> "Rock Summer" took place in Tallinn in June and lasted for three days. The best groups from Estonia were there and many good and interesting groups from Sweden, North-Ireland, Finland, the United Kingdom and the USA. There was every kind of music, from country to punk-rock.
>
> From morning to evening, for three days to end, I heard good music.

Common Threads of Practice

Concerts took place on two stages—one big and one small. There wasn't any pause in the music.

On the big stage played groups from other countries. It's said the main artist of the festival was Robert Cray from the USA. His compositions are a mixture of blues, rock, soul, jazz, and gospel and I enjoyed this mixture.

There played the group, The Jesus and Holy Chain (the UK). Somebody said it was bad but by my mind it was lovely. On the big stage played also some groups from Estonia. For example, "Ultima Thule"—the best Estonian group by my mind.

On the small stage played young groups. I didn't like all these groups but I liked some of them. Punk music isn't good music for girls, but I like punk and hard rock more than disco.

I went to the festival with my friend Kaidi (she is my desk neighbor now) and my cousin Neeve in whose flat in Tallinn we spent the nights.

In the festival were all kinds of people—punks, some hippies, teddy-boys, people with long hair, people without hair, and, of course, decent people (who's a decent person?) with children or without children.

When Pieter Nolvonski—fanciful Estonian actor and singer—sang, one young teddy-boy with hat shouldered me and brought me near the stage. Oh, he was very nice boy by my mind!

From that big snarl of music and crowd I got a striking feeling. I understood—I love summer, music, hamburgers, and crazy young people.

After the end of the concert I had to go home by the train. Next morning I went on an excursion to Lithuania. And I couldn't understand—was it real?

Not every student did such extensive revision, but Liina showed a willingness to produce her best possible piece of writing. In doing this work she improved not only her skills in English but her skills as a writer—in any language.

Ivar was perhaps the student who best internalized my suggestion to convey an idea or feeling by describing a very specific incident. After several drafts and revisions he produced the following piece about an encounter with Americans in Sweden:

In the spring of 1989, when I was in Sweden, I met two boys from California in the United States. It was actually at the time when, after fifty years, the Baltic problem emerged in the world's newspapers, and I told them that I came from Estonia. They, as true Americans, smiled politely and nodded. We went on to talk. But when we finished, Trevor (that was the name of one American boy) asked me, "What is Estonia?" I explained that it's a country that is situated in the northwest of the Soviet Union. The kid again smiled and nodded, but I realized that he didn't understand how one country could be in another. I had to explain that Estonia and the other Baltic states were occupied by the S.U. in 1940. By his nods I decided that he understood me, but a few minuters later he started to tell me how fine the Soviet Army uniform is and called me a friendly "muzik" (fellow) which is known to be specifical Russian word. Now it was my turn to smile and say, "Yes, it is really fine." I wasn't insulted and thought that we have to soon get on the world map in order to be a nation.

This brief story very effectively uses example, understatement, and inference to convey Ivar's frustration at having his national identity swallowed up by the Soviet Union. It symbolizes the much larger issues of Estonian pride and U.S. ignorance and insensitivity to other parts of the world. And it reveals great perception, patience, and determination on the part of the writer. All in a foreign language!

A ninth form student with much weaker English skills also used rewriting to improve her language and refine her ideas. Annika's first ideas, again on a card, read:

> I fie [fear] ve [war] biesor [because] it is a horrow and angry people. I fear stay oloun [alone] hie [here] wizout [without] friends. I not want be autcast [outcast].

This first attempt shows how interwoven her English and Estonian thinking were. She thought in Estonian first, then chose English words that are close to Estonian. She rewrote her sentences on a second card:

> I fear war because it is a horrow, and angry people. I fear stay alone here world without a friends. I not want be outcast. Still I fear dark and between too large expanse. Also own impending life, as I no know what me before expect. I desire these fears not at all know.

In spite of all of the problems with word order and word choice, this piece conveys very strong emotions. In fact, part of the impact is created by unusual word choices such as *expanse* or *impending life*. The question was how to help Annika with English without losing the power of her "voice," a problem even teachers of native speakers must confront.

Annika's fourth and final version of this piece shows what a delicate balance teachers must maintain when they start correcting students' writing:

> All people fear something. A lot depends on the situation. I fear war because it is a horror, and fear bad people. Also I fear staying alone here in the world, without any friends. I do not want to be an outcast. Also I fear the dark and being in a large empty place. Yet I worry about our own

impending life, as I do not know what to expect ahead of me. I fear a broken dreams and unhappy love. I desire to not know these fears at all.

Although this version is not written in perfect English, it is a great improvement over the first try. But many of the changes, some Annika's, some mine, dilute the power of the original. *Bad* is not as specific as *angry*. Was *ahead of me* an improvement over *before me*? *To not know these fears at all* may be correct, but is it as effective as *to know these fears not at all*? And how I miss the *too large expanse*! I regret having emphasized correctness over colorfulness. In the future I would go back to Annika to discuss differences between individual style and conventional usage in an effort to give her informed choices as a writer.

The question of how to respond to "mistakes" and the students' fear of making them was a major concern in my initial sessions. Students expressed great anxiety about their ability to use English. Cynne commented, "I came to school with a little fear in Monday morning, because I had never speak English with foreigners, and I haven't got the practice." A typical Soviet classroom is based on correcting mistakes. The only safe oral statements become those that are carefully prepared and memorized. All my students' previous training led them to believe that they must write and speak perfectly on the first try. Merle wrote, "I did not want to speak English earlier because I was so afraid of making mistakes in my English."

For me as a teacher, mistakes can be important indicators of what students are ready to learn. If students are afraid to make mistakes, they will not take on new challenges with language. If students mask their mistakes, I may be unable to accurately assess their level of development. This does not mean that mistakes are never addressed. After all, these students want to become fluent speakers and not embarrass themselves by appearing ignorant. The question is when to point out errors.

My approach was to let students complete their initial thoughts, whether on paper or in discussion, and to note one or two points to include in a later lesson. In this way we did minilessons on verb placement, tenses, articles, prepositions, and other topics. Written pieces were usually edited on fully developed drafts. Students began to feel more comfortable with this approach. Kaidi wrote, "This week gave me much boldness. Earlier I was afraid to speak English, because I do a lot of mistakes. But now I think that every person study in the mistakes."

In their final evaluations of our work together, students wrote that they found writing in English to be a fruitful avenue for learning the language as well as improving their thinking and writing skills. Astrid wrote:

> Your nice idea to write as much as we can helped me also very much. I'm not afraid of writing in English any more. Probably I don't write better but I've got over the fear. And also the way you made us think—to see and discover good sentences and nice paragraphs, now I can understand how it helps.

And they did write a great deal in a short time. Along with revising drafts, they wrote dialogues in pairs for class performance, pen-pal letters to my New Hampshire students, "goodbye" letters evaluating our class time, and journal entries on nightly reading from paperbacks I had contributed to the class.

Writing About Reading

At the beginning of our session I spread out several dozen books for students to look over and gave thumbnail sketches of most of them. I then asked students to choose a book, read it at home for about an hour each night, and write journal entries about the reading. Many students in the younger class were not embarrassed to choose children's picture books and, in fact, were proud of their ability to later tell the class the story of *Miss Rumphius* (Cooney, 1982), *Grandma's House* (Moore, 1985), or *Cross Country Cat* (Calhoun, 1979). Other students, from both classes, chose challenging books by authors such as John Steinbeck, Aldous Huxley, George Orwell, Ernest Hemingway, and S. E. Hinton. Some, not surprisingly, were able to read only a few chapters in a week and wrote in their journals that they found it slow going with lots of dictionary work, though they enjoyed the chance to read real books in English. Other students, to my pleased amazement, completed the books they chose and started new ones. One boy completed two. If having books in English was a new experience, so was writing about books. Merle wrote, "I write about a book for the first time so I don't know I'll do it right or not."

As with most readers, the students who responded best to their chosen books were those who could personally identify with the contents. Kaidi, who had longed for a puppy and finally got one, fell in love with *Where the Red Fern Grows* (Rawls, 1974). She wrote, "Billy is infected with puppy love. . . . I like this book because I have had also such disease. When I read this book, I live with Billy and remember my

―――――――― **Common Threads of Practice** ――――――――

stories, when I was ten years old." Riina was totally absorbed in *The Outsiders* (Hinton, 1967) and came in daily with lists of words and expressions that she could not find in her dictionary, words such as *c'mon, ain't, greaser, cool,* or *rumble.* When she finished the book, her first words on entering the room were, "It's so sad," but she immediately traded the book in for another by S. E. Hinton, *Rumblefish* (1986). She felt so sorry for Ponyboy that she wrote a letter to him in her journal:

> Dear Ponyboy. You are only fourteen years old, but you have already seen violence and enmity. But you also know what does it mean to have a real friend who are always with you. You haven't got the mother care. You were too young when your parents died. You are fourteen and this is the age, teenagers need parents' advice. You have got only your brothers. And now you are not the most unlucky person although you have lost your best friends. Especially Johnny. Excuse me, you asked everybody not to take this name in our lips. I know, Johnny was and is something very sacred for you, but your life mustn't stop because of somebody's death. You are already so old to make it clear for yourself that your best friend is died.
> Anyway, you have to find your place in that society you have to live. Look for it. You have quite much time to do it and don't forget that you have brothers. Although you three are very different but if you don't have each other, you don't have anything. You have to be able to stick with each other against everything.

Ponyboy was so real and close to Riina that she felt compelled to comfort him and give him advice. Following this letter, Riina wrote these comments:

> When I read the book, I felt something different than I have always felt reading some books. I felt that I was just with them in the book. That I was "greaser" too.... Sometimes I felt that their problems were mine too. I think it is because I felt that I was with them. Although I live in another society, I'm feeling how difficult it is for them to find their place in the crazy world. I hope they do.

For Riina, reading a moving story, learning English, and growing as a person were one, integrated experience.

Students expressed a range of reasons for personal involvement with their books. Cynne was fascinated with *Hiroshima* (Hersey, 1986) because "there are written very little about this event in the Estonian." Merle identified the plight of Native Americans in *When the Legends Die* (Borland, 1963) with that of Estonians:

Teaching English in Estonia

> Both Estonians and Indians are aboriginals of their country but other people have desired their country and they have lost their freedom and land. They like to remember the past when they had a happy days. Both we Estonians and Indians have a danger to become extinct as a nation. But we Estonians feel more hope when we think of the future. I guess Indians have no hope to the better future. That is why I am so sorry for them.

Striking entries came from students who were rebelling against the Soviet system and were reading books satirizing that system. Astrid wrote of *1984* (Orwell, 1984):

> The book I'm reading is really horror-tale. Maybe for Americans and other people from "free world" it's like a nightmare but for Soviet people it is their real past and who knows—perhaps future? Everything in the novel is so familiar—the horror and fear people feel, endless lies, poverty, shame. The mustached paters on every corner looking at you threateningly and all-knowingly. Earsplitting slogans from radio and TV. Philosophy that makes people stupid and dull, anger against culture and humaneness. How could George Orwell forecast the future so exactly? Did he know so much about Stalinism?

Concluding his paper on *Animal Farm* (Orwell, 1956), Kristo wrote, "If I read the book, it's makes me feel bad, but I can't stop the reading. From every page I find something." And of *Brave New World* (Huxley, 1946), he wrote:

> In the conflict of World State destroyed the humanity and freedom, but I think, the Truth couldn't be destroyed. It's stronger than every totalitarian power and state. The hopes of Mr. Savage about New Brave World were fall to dust. I hope not my hopes about future will go the same way.

When I last saw Kristo on a return visit to Estonia in May 1991, he was doing alternative service as a janitor, a practice allowed by the Estonian government but still illegal in the Soviet Union. When the Soviet Army stormed the Vilnius radio station in January to arrest draft resisters, Kristo had hidden in the country for a month in fear that similar reprisals would be taken against Estonian youth. But only 3 months after our visit, his hopes for a free Estonian future were finally realized.

Final Thoughts

Kristo and his Estonian schoolmates had powerful tales to tell the world, tales of family history, personal struggles and triumphs, and their country's suffering and dreams. They are living in a time of radical transitions, able to write thoughts not expressed in Estonia for 40 years. To write these thoughts in what they perceived as the language of freedom was an opportunity they welcomed.

When students are given the chance to write, speak, and read about things that are close to them, they will acquire the skills they need, even in a foreign language. The writing by these Estonian students speaks for itself. They brought me "a draught of fresh water" and "blew me away" with their eagerness to work and learn, and the depth of their thoughts and feelings. I wish these bright, brave young men and women a future as rewarding as all of their best dreams and visions.

References

Borland, H. (1963). *When the legends die.* Philadelphia: Lippincott.

Calhoun, M. (1979). *Cross country cat.* New York: Morrow.

Cooney, B. (1982). *Miss Rumphuis.* New York: Viking.

Hersey, J. (1986). *Hiroshima.* New York: Bantam.

Hinton, S. E. (1967). *The outsiders.* New York: Viking.

Hinton, S. E. (1986). *Rumblefish.* New York: Dell.

Huxley, A. (1946). *Brave new world.* New York: Harper.

Moore, E. (1985). *Grandma's house.* New York: Lothrop, Lee, & Shepard.

Orwell, G. (1956). *Animal farm.* New York: New American Library.

Orwell, G. (1984). *1984.* San Diego: Harcourt Brace Jovanovich.

Rawls, W. (1974). *Where the red fern grows.* New York: Bantam.

Teacher Resources

This list of resources is designed for teachers interested in reading more about some of the methods and techniques described in the chapters in this book. The list is not exhaustive; it is a sampler of materials that we use and like.

Atwell, Nancie. (1987). *In the middle: Writing, reading and learning with adolescents.* Portsmouth, NH: Boynton/Cook.

> Written by a former eighth-grade English teacher who replaced her traditional English teaching approaches with extremely successful writing and reading workshops, the book is theoretically sound and full of practical suggestions for teachers at all grade levels, not just the middle school grades. Atwell writes well, and her love of books and writing, as well as her respect for learners, resounds.

Baskwill, J., & Whitman, P. (1988). *Evaluation: Whole language, whole child.* New York: Scholastic.

> This book is devoted to alternative assessment strategies, many of which are appropriate for writing workshop (e.g., anecdotal records, interviews, surveys).

Bird, Lois Bridges. (1989). *Becoming a whole language school: The Fair Oaks story.* Katonah, NY: Richard C. Owens.

> Fair Oaks School, located in northern California, USA, serves a predominantly language minority community. This book, written primarily by Fair Oaks teachers, describes their odyssey from skill-based to meaning-based learning and teaching.

Calkins, Lucy McCormick. (1986). *The art of teaching writing.* Portsmouth, NH: Heinemann.

> This highly readable book combines research and practice. Chapters deal with children changing as writers, writing conferences, the role of the teacher, writing across the curriculum, and the connection between reading and writing.

Edelsky, Carole. (1986). *Writing in a bilingual program: Había una vez*. Norwood, NJ: Ablex.

> Edelsky argues for authentic writing opportunities, basing her discussion and recommendations on her longitudinal study of the writing development of children in a bilingual school.

Goodman, Kenneth S., Goodman, Yetta M., & Hood, Wendy J. (Eds.). (1989). *The whole language evaluation book*. Portsmouth, NH: Heinemann.

> A major concern of many educators who are interested in whole language is evaluation. This book is one of the few that deal with the issue. The articles are written by teachers (of Grades K–12) who describe how they evaluate in the classroom.

Graves, Donald. (1983). *Writing: Teachers and children at work*. Portsmouth, NH: Heinemann.

> This very practical and highly readable book is intended for teachers who want to establish writing workshops. Topics include how to establish a writing workshop, how to conduct conferences, when and how to teach skills, how children develop as writers, and how to record children's growth.

Graves, Donald. (1989). *Experiment with fiction*. Portsmouth, NH: Heinemann.

> When children write fiction, their stories often lack plausibility and cohesion. Graves gives concrete suggestions for helping children to become better fiction writers.

Graves, Donald. (1989). *Investigate non-fiction*. Portsmouth, NH: Heinemann.

> Graves shows how teachers can help students write nonfiction (e.g., letters and reports) that builds on their knowledge of the world around them.

Graves, Donald. (1990). *Discover your own literacy*. Portsmouth, NH: Heinemann.

> How many teachers are responsible for reading and writing development? Of these teachers, how many read and write and share their literacy with their students? Graves paints a very compelling picture of the need to do so.

Hall, Nigel. (1989). *Writing with reason*. Portsmouth, NH: Heinemann.

> Hall focuses on how children between the ages of 3 and 7 function as authors. Many of the chapters are written by British classroom teachers.

Teacher Resources

Harste, Jerome C., & Short, Kathy G. (1988). *Creating classrooms for authors: The reading-writing connection.* Portsmouth, NH: Heinemann.

This book is a practical guide to teachers who would like to organize process-oriented (whole language) classrooms. Clearly presented theoretical rationales and instructional alternatives accompany classroom activities.

Heald-Taylor, Gail. (1986). *Whole language strategies for ESL students.* Toronto, Ontario, Canada: OISE Press.

Heald-Taylor describes a variety of whole language–related learning events and classroom activities. It has more of a "recipe book" flavor to it than do many of the other books listed here.

Heard, Georgia. (1989). *For the good earth and sun: Teaching poetry.* Portsmouth, NH: Heinemann.

Heard, a poet who has worked extensively with children, invites teachers to immerse children in poetry as readers and writers.

ILEA (Inner London Education Authority) Centre for Primary Education. (1988). *The primary language record: Handbook for teachers.* Portsmouth, NH: Heinemann.

Contains some excellent suggestions for informally recording children's language and literacy development.

Newman, Judith M. (Ed.) (1985). *Whole language: Theory in use.* Portsmouth, NH: Heinemann.

The chapters in this highly readable book, many written by practicing teachers in Canada, describe how teachers have applied whole language theory to their classrooms. They stress how reading and writing can become a way to help people to understand the world better.

Peyton, Joy Kreeft, & Reed, Leslee. (1990). *Dialogue journal writing with nonnative English speakers: A handbook for teachers.* Alexandria, VA: Teachers of English to Speakers of Other Languages.

The authors offer a comprehensive overview of what a dialogue journal is, discuss the role of dialogue journals in the classroom, and show how to introduce dialogue journals and keep them going.

Rigg, Pat, & Allen, Virginia (Eds). (1989). *When they don't all speak English.* Urbana, IL: National Council of Teachers of English.

Rigg and Allen provide helpful advice for teachers who have never taught ESOL learners. The chapters provide an overview of integrated language teaching, particularly in classroom settings in which native and nonnative English speakers are combined for instruction.

Common Threads of Practice

Rigg, Pat, & Enright, D. Scott (Eds.). (1986). *Children and ESL: Integrating perspectives*. Alexandria, VA: Teachers of English to Speakers of Other Languages.

The seven chapters discuss ways in which all facets of language are interconnected. The authors share the belief that language is best learned and taught in an integrated, authentic way.

Turbill, Jan (Ed.). (1982). *No better way to teach writing!* Rozelle, New South Wales, Australia: Primary English Teaching Association (distributed in the United States by Heinemann).

Turbill relates how Australian teachers and children in the elementary grades established a process approach to writing. Although the major focus is on children in the first three grades, teachers of older children also contribute insights and perspectives. A sequel, *Now, We Want to Write!* is available.

Weaver, Constance. (1988). *Reading process and practice: From psycholinguistics to whole language*. Portsmouth, NH: Heinemann.

Weaver presents a comprehensive and highly readable discussion of the reading process.

About the Editors

Katharine Davies Samway is Associate Professor in the College of Education at San José State University, San José, California. She is a former chair of the ESOL in Elementary Education Interest Section of TESOL and is Associate Editor of the *TESOL Journal*. She writes frequently about the language and literacy development of children acquiring English as a nonnative language.

Denise McKeon is Outreach Manager for the National Clearinghouse for Bilingual Education in Washington, DC. She is a former Chair of the ESOL in Elementary Education Interest Section of TESOL and is the Chair of the TESOL Task Force on Policy and Standards for Language Minority Students (K–12) in the United States. She writes frequently about program design and policy issues.

Also available from TESOL

All Things to All People:
A Primer for K-12 ESL Teachers in Small Programs
Donald C. Flemming, Lucie C. Germer, and Christiane Kelley

A World of Books:
An Annotated Reading List for ESL/EFL Students
Dorothy S. Brown

Children and ESL: Integrating Perspectives
Pat Rigg and D. Scott Enright, Editors

Coherence in Writing:
Research and Pedagogical Perspectives
Ulla Connor and Ann Johns, Editors

Dialogue Journal Writing with Nonnative English Speakers:
A Handbook for Teachers
Joy Kreeft Peyton and Leslee Reed

Dialogue Journal Writing with Nonnative English Speakers:
An Instructional Packet for Teachers and Workshop Leaders
Joy Kreeft Peyton and Jana Staton

Directory of Professional Preparation Programs
in TESOL in the United States, 1992–1994
Helen Kornblum, with Ellen Garshick, Editors

Diversity as Resource:
Redefining Cultural Literacy
Denise E. Murray, Editor

A New Decade of Language Testing Research:
Selected Papers From the 1990 Language Testing Research
Colloquium
Dan Douglas and Carol Chapelle, Editors

New Ways in Teaching Reading
Richard R. Day, Editor

New Ways in Teacher Education
Donald Freeman, with Steve Cornwell, Editors

Research in Reading in English as a Second Language
Joanne Devine, Patricia L. Carrell, and David E. Eskey, Editors

*Students and Teachers Writing Together:
Perspectives on Journal Writing*
Joy Kreeft Peyton, Editor

*Video in Second Language Teaching:
Using, Selecting, and Producing Video for the Classroom*
Susan Stempleski and Paul Arcario, Editors

For more information, contact
Teachers of English to Speakers of Other Languages, Inc.
1600 Cameron Street, Suite 300
Alexandria, Virginia 22314 USA
Tel 703-836-0774 ▪ Fax 703-836-7864